All
the
Best –
Liz
Weber

Don't Let 'Em Treat You Like™ A GIRL

A Woman's Guide to Leadership Success

(Tips from the Guys)

By

Liz Weber

Don't Let 'Em Treat You Like™
A GIRL
A Woman's Guide to Leadership Success
(Tips from the Guys)
by Liz Weber

Book Surge, LLC, 5341 Dorchester Road,
Suite 16, North Charleston, SC 29418 USA

http://www.DontLetEmTreatYouLikeAGirl.com
http://www.liz-weber.com/products.htm

ISBN: 1-59109-981-1

Warning – Disclaimer

This publication is designed to provide competent and reliable information regarding the subject matter. However, it is sold with the understanding that the author and publisher are not rendering specific legal, financial, or other professional advice. Laws and practices often vary from state to state; therefore, if you need legal or other expert assistance, seek the services of a professional. The author and publisher specifically disclaim any liability that might be incurred from the use or application of the contents of this book.

Every effort has been made to make this book as accurate as possible. However, mistakes are possible, both typographical and in content. Therefore, this text should be used only as a general guide and not as the ultimate source for professional and leadership behavior. Also, this book contains statistics that have been approved by the originating sources.

It is not the intent of this book to encapsulate all relevant information available on professionalism, body language, business etiquette, communication skills, women's leadership, leadership in general, or any of the topics addressed herein. You are urged to research, read, and observe others to learn as much as you can on any of the topics most interesting or most important to you.

This book's purpose is to educate and entertain. The author and publisher are neither liable nor responsible to any person or entity with respect to any loss or damage caused, or alleged to have been caused, directly or indirectly, by the information contained in this book.

If you do not wish to be bound by the above, you may return the book to the publisher for a full refund.

Table of Contents

Note to the Reader

Professional opportunities for everyone, men and women, are more bountiful than ever. With constantly changing technologies, spin-off and virtual businesses, the opportunities to make your professional dreams a reality are now more possible than ever before. This book's intent is to help clue you in to the subtle, and not-so-subtle, behavioral traits needed to more effectively interact in a professional arena and to be treated like the professional you are.

Most of my observations, ideas, tips, and suggestions are gained from my years of experience working in male-dominated environments. To help clarify my thoughts for those who struggle with being viewed as a professional equal, I requested and received stories, tips, and words of wisdom from many kind contributors. Their stories and my own are included here to help spur ideas and awareness on how you can better interact professionally with those around you.

I have also included quotations from experts on behavior and leadership, as well as some of my own thoughts. The highlighted comments without attribution, are mine.

If after reading the book, and possibly sharing a copy with a friend, you've identified and experienced ways *not* to be treated like a girl, let me know. Send your comments and thoughts to me at: *info@liz-weber.com* Thanks and enjoy.

Liz Weber

Dedication

This book is dedicated to my parents, LeRoy and Frances Weber.

To help you understand these two special people, I'll let my sister Pat's words describe them for you. Here's part of her reply to my request for words of wisdom:

Part of growing up in our family was working with Dad. He ran his own business and with so many children, we became his work force. Working with Dad was the most exhilarating and the most frightening experience in the world. I don't think he ever really realized the tremendous impact he made on shaping the work ethic of his children. Dad was a tough taskmaster. He was doing very important work with very inexperienced help. No matter what the particular job on any given day, Dad was the main man and we were the grunts. He expected everyone that worked with him, "to be one step ahead of me." Until you wised up, it could be a long time until lunch!

Dad had so much common sense that he truly didn't understand why anyone couldn't "get it." If he was laying pipe in a trench, you were expected to watch him so closely that you could anticipate his next move and have the tool ready for him before he even knew it. Working with Dad was like performing surgery – the teamwork between the doctor and the surgical staff is so critical to a successful operation. That "teamwork" we learned from watching Mom work with Dad. She respected his strengths and he respected hers. They were so busy raising thirteen kids and running their own business that I truly think they "accepted the best" about each other and "forgot the rest" on a daily basis.

Because they had a real zest for life, they both started the day on their knees, then jumped up, and hit the ground at a dead run. Dad always said he couldn't wait to get up every day. Every day was a new adventure. I rarely remember either of them being in a "bad" mood. We, as children, had the gift of being wanted and we felt it. As we became teenagers, my heart goes out to them for having lived through it.

So, I think two things have stuck so tight with me that they are a part of me. One is, "think ahead." I always try to weave my way through a project considering all possibilities. This trait leaves a trail of its own: pay attention to details; be organized, efficient, and thorough. The second is to consider each day a "new adventure." As I get older, I realize, it truly is. Each day offers so many possibilities. What we make of our day is our choice.

Thanks Mom and Dad!

I agree. Thanks Mom and Dad.

Acknowledgements

I'd like to thank the many contributors who graciously shared their insights: Patti Anfang, Susanne Cardella, Holli Catchpole, Jim Cathcart, Joseph Colucci, Margaret Duncan, Dan Fisher, Sam Horn, Terry McGee, Deirdre Morgan, Dr. Sheila Murray-Bethel, Christine Oxley, Robert Oxley, Ed Price, Susana Ramirez, Gina Schreck, Deb Sofield, Colleen Stanley, and Bill Weber. Your input helped this book have the real-person perspective I wanted. The readers and I are indebted to you.

Thank you also to Business Women's Network, Center for Women's Business Research, National Association for Female Executives, Society for Human Resource Management, and The Employment Policy Foundation for your support.

Special thanks to Pat Anfang, Karen Bitner, Dana Given, Suzanne Harvey, and Frances Weber for your editing talents, and to Dina Snow of Azteca Design for the cover design.

And, as always, thanks Bob. Without your constant support and refocusing talks, this book would not have happened.

Section 1 - The Background
(for those who want it)

As long as you agree to fulfill a leadership role, accept that responsibility and that challenge. Because in the workplace, that's the role you want to be judged on – not your "woman-ness."

Why There's ANOTHER Book on Leadership Success for Women

This book is written with the hope that it can help one woman.

A thirty-something woman stopped me after my presentation at the American Business Women's Association's National Convention in Albuquerque a few years ago. She had waited quietly, off to one side, while I talked with several attendees. As the crowd thinned, she approached me a bit hesitantly, offered me her fingertips to shake, and said timidly, "I could never do what you do. You're so confident and powerful. I'm the manager of a real estate office. I work really hard and I'd like to move up in the company, but I don't have a degree. My manager doesn't respect me. He says I need to be more professional. I guess I'm not leadership material because I care too much for people. I don't know what to do."

I was stunned. In that one interaction, she had done and said so many things that were so fundamentally "girly." First, the hesitant way she had approached me immediately told me she wasn't a confident woman. Second, she was limiting herself and her abilities by saying, "I could never do what you do." With that mindset, she was pre-determining her future. If she was going to limit herself, then she was also going to lose the right to grumble when her current situation never changed. Third, her manager wanted her to be more professional and didn't seem to respect her. I got the impression she thought it was his responsibility to help her become a "professional." Wrong. It's her responsibility – no one else's – to advance her career. And fourth, why did she think being a leader meant not caring about people? If anything, it's the complete opposite. Real leaders focus on and develop their people. They realize their employees' skills and abilities will determine how well their organizations grow. If they expect to grow organizations, they have to develop people. Caring for and developing people is crucial to leadership.

Also, as she had been talking, I had noticed her eyes darted from me to the right, left, down, back to me, then left, and back down.

She couldn't hold eye contact with me. She was an attractive woman, but she accentuated her femaleness more than her professionalism. She had long blonde hair with billowing curls reminiscent of the Farrah Fawcett 1970's just-tumbled-out-of-bed hairdo. Her chest was covered – well *more* of it could have been covered – by a white blouse with big ruffles running down the front. She wore a hot-pink suit jacket and a matching hot-pink skirt – tight. She had great legs that were nicely accentuated by the matching three-inch, hot-pink, spiked heels on her feet. What you couldn't help but notice, whether you were a man or a woman, was her womanly shape. She had a great body and her clothing accentuated every curve. Needless to say, what she accentuated got noticed.

When she asked me what she could do to start earning the respect of her manager and co-workers, my first, unpolished words were, "Stop acting like a girl." As I said those words, I remembered hearing similar words of wisdom from my dad when I was 24. I had called him for advice as I had prepared to negotiate my first *new* car purchase. After I had reviewed my research on the car with him, he had said, "You know what to do. Now don't let 'em treat you like a girl." When I had heard that, I was shocked. Naively, I had never thought I would be treated differently because I'm female. But Dad's words had struck a chord with me. He had never said anything like that before, and he had a great deal more experience than I in making major purchases, so there had to be something to this.

As I had absorbed his advice, I realized this comment was his way of telling me: *Be an adult. Be smart. Be prepared. Think ahead. Stand your ground. Don't allow yourself to be ignorant of the facts. Don't go into this negotiation process unprepared like a naïve girl.* Dad wasn't speaking of sexism per-se. He was telling me I couldn't act like a girl and expect the sales person to take care of me and to make a good deal for me. If I did, the salesperson *would* take advantage of me. It wouldn't be personal; it'd be business. The salesperson's job is to sell cars at a profit for the dealership. It's my job as the customer to make an informed purchase.

Now many years later, Dad's advice was coming from my mouth. This woman hadn't acted confident; she hadn't looked terribly professional; and she hadn't presented herself as a confident professional. Therefore, she wasn't being treated as a confident professional. Even if she had dressed more conservatively, she still would have projected "girly-girl" because of her demeanor. She would still be treated like a girl. She would be treated as others viewed her.

Following that exchange, I realized that if this woman wasn't aware of her "girly" behaviors, other women were probably unaware of theirs too. That could be why so many women are unhappy with their careers and have strained relationships with their male and female colleagues. With that in mind, I contacted everyone in my data base, female and male, as well as many other people, and asked for their insights on what women do that prevents them from being viewed as professionals or as equals in the workplace. What had they done, experienced, seen, or been taught that they could share with others to help women (and some men) no longer act, and therefore, be treated like "girls"?

The responses were enlightening, humorous, confirming, and honest. To all of my contributors, thanks. Your insights could well help someone behave and be treated like the professional, like the leader, she or he wants to be.

This book does *not* provide and then elaborate on the essential qualities of a leader. Honestly, that information is available in a number of other publications. This is not an "I hate men" book nor is it a "Life isn't fair because I'm a woman" book.

Many of the ideas I share in this book apply to men as well as women. It is for women *and* men who believe they're "stuck." It is for women and men who believe they cannot reach their vision of professional success because others don't support them or others haven't provided them with opportunities to be successful.

This book's intent is to demonstrate for those of you who feel stuck that you sometimes do things yourselves that limit your professional and leadership opportunities. If you want to be viewed as a professional, or as a leader, be aware of the signals you're sending.

Our world is a world in which men and women work together – a mixed workplace. It's diversity of the first order. Men and women innately think differently, but when we work in the same business culture, we all have to abide by the cultural norms of the organization. And yes, that might well mean women have to be a bit less womanly, but men have to be a bit less manly too. The guys have to cut the macho crap, and we women have to cut the "girly" stuff. Basically, we all need to be aware of and control our behaviors that can cause disruption, confusion, or conflict in the workplace. If we all can agree to that, the workplace is a much more enjoyable and productive place to be.

Changing Times

The U.S. Department of Labor projects that by 2010, 48% of the American workforce will be composed of women. As reported by The Employment Policy Foundation in Washington, women hold nearly half of all managerial and professional positions in the U.S. workplace and will hold about 54% of these jobs by 2030. That means more and more women will be presented with leadership opportunities. As evidence of this trend, the 2002 gubernatorial races had the highest number of women candidates ever – 21 of 36 races.

Also, the Center for Women's Business Research data shows:

(1)   Between 1997 and 2002,
        a. the number of women-owned
            firms increased by 14% nation-
            wide – twice the rate of all
            firms;
        b. the employment numbers in
            women-owned firms increased
            by 30% – one and one-half
            times the U.S. rate; and
        c. the sales by women-owned
            firms grew by 40%.
(2)   Women-owned firms continue to
        diversify into all industries. Con-
        struction, transportation, agricultural
        services, communications, and pub-
        lic utilities have seen the largest re-
        cent increases in the number of
        women-owned firms.

What does this mean? To me it indicates
that women, now more than ever, need to
understand how to better "fit in," how to
"play the game," and how to be equal players in the professional arena. Many women
do this flawlessly, naturally, and without
losing any of their femininity. Other women
(and men) seem to struggle. It's for them,
and for the woman in Albuquerque, for
those who don't understand why they're
treated like girls, that this project took
shape.

My insights and those of my contributors come from working in various environments including global organizations, small mom and pop shops, start-ups, manufacturing facilities, financial institutions, organizations that were male-dominated, organizations that were female-dominated, as well as various federal, state, and county government agencies.

Tips from the Guys

As the title of the book indicates, many of the more practical and honest bits of advice came directly or indirectly from men. More often than not, the men shared advice that was so blunt – yet so insightful – I was amazed. They very clearly articulated their observations, appreciation of, and frustrations in working with, supervising, and being managed by women.

I am by no means suggesting that the female contributors' input was less valuable. I was simply struck with how honest and open the men's input was. There was no anti-female angle to it. It was shared to clue women in on how to be treated like professional equals. Contrary to popular belief, the guys aren't trying to keep women out of or down in the professional world. If anything, they're trying to help women advance. Men know the data I shared above. They know and see the predominance of women in the workplace. Because of this, men want women to work with them in growing the organizations where they work. The more we help each other, the more we all succeed.

> *Contrary to popular belief, the guys aren't trying to keep women out or down in the professional world. If anything, they're trying to help women advance. Men know the data I shared above. They know and see the predominance of women in the workplace. Because of this, men want women to work with them in growing the organizations where they work. The more we help each other, the more we all succeed.*

Also, the words of wisdom that most resonated with many of my female respondents was advice they'd received from their husbands, fathers, brothers, grandfathers, male bosses, or male colleagues. Finally, given the dominance of men in leadership positions, it's only logical to watch them, learn from them, and identify what they do that works. This is how many of my female contributors gained their insights. Now, it's up to us to adapt and apply these ideas, techniques, and insights, and to make them work for us as well.

Sometimes We Get What We Ask for

> *"Sometimes people treat us the way they do not because of the way they are, but because of the way we are."*
> TONGUE FU'ISM
> Sam Horn, Author and Originator of
> *Tongue Fu!*®

I'm walking on dangerous ground here, but I have to be blunt: Girls do a lot of dumb things (boys do too, but we're talking about girls here). Their stereotypical and self-defeating behaviors are fading. However, many girls (most prevalently teenage girls) are incredibly insecure, believe their worth and value is determined by their looks, readily belittle themselves, know they're smart but don't stand up for themselves, need to talk to one another frequently for validation, and doubt themselves constantly. Hey, I know. I lived it. I also grew up with five sisters and I've raised two daughters. It's ugly but it's the truth. Thankfully, most of us grow out of it.

As adults, however, women often default to some of these same self-defeating behaviors. When that happens, women emit silent signals to others that they're not confident women, but insecure girls. And honestly, no one likes following someone who's insecure. It's downright frightening. Because of these silent signals, women sabotage their own attempts at professional or leadership success. How? If "the boss" is considering a woman for a promotion or a lead position on a particular project, but then sees her second-guessing herself, backing away from her original position, or worrying more about her fingernail appliqués than about getting the job done, "the boss" has a right to question her leadership abilities.

So how do you resolve this? Identify what you might be doing that is sending the wrong or conflicting signals about your professional abilities. If you want to be viewed as a professional – as a leader – you need to be aware of the signals you're sending.

> *If "the boss" is considering a woman for a promotion or a lead position on a particular project, but then sees her second-guessing herself, backing away from her original position, or worrying more about her fingernail appliqués than about getting the job done, "the boss" has a right to question her leadership abilities.*

We ARE Women – But What's Our JOB?

I think by now you get my point. I'm in no way suggesting that we should deny our womanhood and not look or act like women in the workplace. I'm suggesting that when we take our "femaleness" a bit too far, it becomes our defining character point. It also frankly becomes a distraction. Being a woman then takes precedence over being a doctor, receptionist, CEO, or committee chair. This is no different than focusing more on being Jewish than on being a Senior Programmer. Your responsibility, while you're working as a Senior Programmer, technician, or sales associate, is to do that job. The fact that you're Jewish, or a woman, is simply that – a fact. Be proud of it. Be proud of being an African-American or whatever your race. Be proud of your age. Be proud of who you are. But then remember, in the workplace or in any other situation in which you are expected to provide guidance and leadership, your responsibility as a leader is to be a leader. The people who put you in that position and the people who support you in that position expect you to do the job, to fulfill its responsibilities, and to fulfill the role. So if you're a woman who is a 58-year-old Jewish, African-American – good for you. But as long as you agree to fulfill a leadership role, accept that responsibility and that challenge. Because in the workplace, that's the role you want to be judged on – not your "woman-ness."

Carly Fiorina, the CEO of Hewlett-Packard, is known to demand that she be judged as a leader, not as a woman. Why? It's her job to be the CEO. She knows she's a woman. We know she's a woman. We can see that. But can she lead? That's the challenge for her because that's the responsibility she's accepted. Now it's her job to behave as a leader while she has that responsibility.

And this is exactly where many of us run into problems. Whether we aspire to lead a global company like Hewlett-Packard or to lead our local homeowners' association, there are specific professional skills and traits that are required in both arenas. It's our job to identify and exhibit them.

Oh My Gosh! I've Done That!

I have to be honest – as my contributors' survey responses started to return, there were a few moments when I caught myself saying, "Oh my gosh! I've done that!" Even though I've worked comfortably and well with men for years, I started to see how some of my well-intentioned behaviors could be viewed as "girly."

Not any one of my or the other "girly" behaviors I'll cover in this book is terribly wrong. Yet, when combined with others, they can send some pretty self-defeating messages.

With that in mind, I hope you can find a few, "Oh my gosh! I've done that!" insights on the pages ahead. Together, let's identify our self-defeating behaviors. Then, if we choose to, we can take control of our lives and become the professionals, the leaders, and the "successes" we want to be.

> *If we want to be viewed as professionals – as leaders – we need to be aware of the signals we're sending.*

Section 2 – The Tips
(for those who want to get to the point)

Don't think that the top position is THE leadership position. It's often a bunch of problems with authority, control, politics, and power. Men have found out that it's not always as great being at the top as they thought it would be.

Tip # 1 - Figure Out What You Want

Grab onto your dream and get your vision of that dream crystal clear. When you see it as clearly as you see the piles of work on your desk, you will begin to make that dream a reality. Regardless of what other people may say to discourage you, focus on the dream. No matter how "far out" your dreams may seem, if you keep your focus clear, they will begin to move into the realm of reality.
Gina Schreck, author of *Marriage Mechanics, Inside Out Success,* and *10 Steps to Become a Pessimist*

You're probably hoping to learn the secret to leadership success in this book. That could be one of the reasons you bought this book: The subtitle says, "A Woman's Guide to Leadership Success."

So what is "Leadership Success"? I don't know. I mean, I can't tell you what it means to you, but I do know what it means to me.

And what it means to me should be irrelevant to you.

To achieve "Leadership Success" you need to identify what it means to *you*. Then pursue *that*. Does it mean the top spot? Does it mean financial security, a hefty salary, an impressive title, the corner office, being the ultimate authority, being involved, being the decision-maker, being a role model for someone, or does it simply mean enjoying your job, being fulfilled by it, and then walking away at the end of the day to your *other life*?

Take a moment and jot down your answers to these statements I often ask my clients to complete:

1. *If I were a leader, I would no longer*

    _____

    _____.

2. *I'll know I'm a leader when*

    _____

    _____.

3. *Being a success will allow me to*

    _____

    _____.

You might be surprised at your answers. Your answers might reveal that your view of success is very much tied to financial rewards, titles, positions, or other people's perceptions. Or, your answers might tell you that what you view as success has nothing to do with money, power, or titles at all. Instead your success is centered around comfortable, solid relationships and helping others. Whatever your answers indicate, there are no wrong answers. Your answers are *your* answers and they are your answers at this point in your life. Because your answers might be different than what you intellectually believe leadership success is, you might be struggling with your current level of success. What you think you want is not what you really want. Then, when you're not satisfied with what you have, your lack of self-confidence kicks in.

I've seen people who believe they want the power, money, and top spot, when what they really want is the self-confidence and financial contentedness they see in those they view as successful. You don't need to have a lot of money to be financially content and self-confident. You just have to know what amount of financial wealth will make you content and identify why you lack self-confidence. Financial contentedness for some of you could be a few thousand dollars; for others, it could be a few hundred million. Whatever it is, it is.

Because most people have never really stopped and seriously thought about this, they don't really know what they want or what will make them feel "successful." They don't know what they're working towards. They don't know if they're making progress or spinning their wheels. They never achieve "it," so they're never really content. They just know they're not where they want to be.

A young married woman with three small children decided to become an independent Mary Kay® sales consultant. When I asked her why, she replied, "I want to have enough money so when I go to the grocery store, I can buy two loaves of bread right away instead of just one." Her comment struck me. Not only did it highlight the true state of her family's finances, but it also clearly stated what "success" would look like to her. Her "success" would be to alleviate, at a bare minimum, that one financial worry she faced each week. With that level of clarity in her mind, she had a much greater chance to reach her vision of success. She did – and she exceeded it. In just over one year, she had recruited her own team of over 20 Sales Associates and became a Director with Mary Kay®.

Identify what your vision of "Leadership Success" is. See "it" in your mind's eye. Once you know what "it" is, realize there will never be a clear, straight shot to "it." However, once you know what you want, you can minimize the really far-out tangents. As one of my contributors said, *"Be willing to compromise on the tactics in the pursuit of the prize."* Not being flexible in how you ultimately achieve your success will only provide roadblocks and slow your progress. Remember, we learn by the little tangents we have to take every now and then. We learn by having to look for opportunities in the world around us.

You Don't Need to Be the CEO to Be a Leader

By working faithfully eight hours a day you may eventually get to be the boss and work twelve hours a day.

Robert Frost

There's nothing more irritating than hearing a woman say, "I'm only support staff," or "I'm just a bookkeeper." Do you know what you're saying? As support staff, you are the hub that holds your office together! As a bookkeeper, you are helping to ensure the money is coming into and going out of the company in a controlled fashion. How can you not see how crucial your work is? You don't need to be in the top spot to be a leader or a success.

A theme that came across as I interviewed and discussed this topic with some of my male contributors was: Don't think that the top position is THE leadership position. It's often a bunch of problems with authority, control, politics, and power. Men have found out that it's not always as great being at the top as they thought it would be.

A leader is someone others respect and want to work with and work for. That ability can reside in all tiers of an organization – not just the top spots.

> *You don't need to be in the top spot to be a leader or a success.*

After I graduated college, I started my career as an intern with the U.S. Department of State. After my summer internship ended, I joined the office as a contracted "Program Analyst," which was a jazzy term for Administrative Assistant. In that role, I experienced first-hand the power the administrative staff carries. The office I worked for was very small, but provided support to roughly 30,000 Americans living and working at the American Embassies and Consulates around the world. Looking back, I had tremendous power at a very young age. My boss came to me *to get things done*. I became the "go-to" person. As the lead person on the support staff, my work in developing briefs, correspondence, speeches, reports, etc., was crucial. I had to dig through files, gather and analyze data, present synopses, and interact with customers, staff, and other agency personnel. As my understanding of how to do the work increased, my ability to see the big picture increased. I knew why things were the way they were. I knew the history, the data, and the interconnections of the players. Because of my work, promotions followed, and my boss relied more and more on my opinions and advice. More importantly, others outside the office also came to know me as the "go-to" person. My staff and I were young, but we earned the respect of others and made things happen.

I never fully realized the reputation I had established as *the* "go-to" person, until ten years after I'd left that position. I had long since started my own business and was in Denver International Airport, when I recognized a man at an adjacent ticket counter. He had owned a prominent law firm in Washington, D.C., and had served as outside legal counsel to my office at the State Department. I had worked with him and his colleagues on a daily basis. When I reintroduced myself to him, he stared at me with that look that indicated he knew me but was having a hard time fully recalling me from his memory banks. Needless to say, I didn't belabor the point and I went on my way. However, later as I was walking to my gate, he spotted me and pulled the young man standing next to him toward me. When they approached he said, "Liz, I apologize. Seeing you brought back so many memories. They all flashed through my mind at once. Anyway, I'd like my son to meet you." Upon exchanging niceties, his son said to me, "It's a pleasure meeting you. I'd heard about you for years. Dad used to talk about this young woman who managed so many responsibilities and wielded so much power in an organization dominated by gray-haired men. Not many people could have done what you did at such a young age." I had had the power – but I never had the top spot.

Understand the Power Your Position Carries

Understanding the power your position carries is crucial. Years ago I attended a businesswomen's dinner. As the members took turns introducing themselves to me, time and again, I'd hear a member say something such as, "I'm Karen Smith and I'm just the Produce Manager at Groceries R Us." By saying, "I'm *just* the Produce Manager" she gave very little credibility or importance to that position or her expertise. In many grocery stores, the produce manager is the final authority in determining which produce is stocked and which isn't to generate the greatest produce sales volume. To do that well, the produce manager requires a solid knowledge of such things as customer purchasing patterns and preferences, product quality and availability, and vendor pricing. Given her ability to determine what and when produce is marketed, purchased and stocked, the produce manager can influence the buying patterns of customers. That isn't something that *just* anyone can do well.

Now, working with organizational restructuring clients, I regularly remind them: "You have the personnel positions you have for a reason. Each position has a specific set of responsibilities that it needs to fulfill to allow the organization to succeed. If those tasks and responsibilities are essential to the organization, then we need the position. If they're not, we don't need that position. Most organizations can't afford to have 'fluff' positions or carry excess staff."

Therefore, the position you have *is* necessary; it *is* important. Because it's important, do it to the best of your ability. If you're in the number one spot, be the best number one you can be. If you're in the newest entry-level spot, be the best entry-level employee you can be.

You have to prove yourself capable of handling and understanding the value of the responsibilities of whatever position you hold. That's what a solid professional does. That's what others admire. That's leadership.

> *I've never wanted the CEO job. I don't*
> *think I have the talents for it.   I'm*
> *a great No. 2 person.*
> Colleen Barrett, President & COO –
> Southwest Airlines

The skills needed to perform at any level are for all intents and purposes – "tools." They are the tools that will help get things done. As people move into leadership roles, their toolbox needs to change. Leaders, most obviously, politicians and executives, rely more and more on their networks, relationships, communication skills, and political savvy to get things done. Their ability to be involved with and direct the office politics will determine their success at getting things done.

Tip # 2 - It's a Game. There's a Strategy. Know the Rules.

By game, I don't mean this isn't serious stuff. I mean there's a strategy to being a professional, to being a leader, and to being a success. You just have to figure out the strategy. Then you can "play."

Here are "The Rules" according to Susanne Cardella, District Manager, On-Premise Southern Wine & Spirits of Colorado:

You have to understand that men started this business game. It is a game and they made the rules. The rules, obviously, come from a male perspective. Women and men think differently. Although being different doesn't mean one is right or wrong – but it does lead to misunderstandings in the workplace.

Rule #1
No emotions allowed (except anger). Women have been taught it's OK to let people know how you feel about everything. "The Rules" state that professionalism

means being stoic. Men punch walls out of frustration; women cry. Crying is taboo because men don't do it. Women are also used to venting all of their problems. To men, this comes across as a whiny, bad attitude. Men don't want to hear it or work through issues as a team. They want it done the way they asked for it – without discussion.

Rule #2
Men are respected for being tough and aggressive. Women are considered to be bitchy under the exact same circumstances. Most women don't believe they have to be a hard-ass to get the job done. Many women believe management is better executed through psychology than intimidation. This often makes women seem weak because they want to talk about issues, where men just want decisions. Also, if you happen to be attractive or petite, you've got an even bigger mountain to climb. Men are ingrained to protect such women – not follow their orders.

Rule #3
Men bond with men. Women bond with women. Unfortunately, the people in power to promote are generally men. Therefore, women don't often have the relationships

with the key people in their company who can help them. Even if you're "buddies" with a man in power, you will NEVER be able to relate to each other as if you were the same sex. You cannot be in the boys' club without being a boy. You can play on the fringe but you will not enter the inner sanctum.

Rule #4
Most men consider their careers to be their lives and identity. Most women believe that their job does not define who they are. They have family and friends and other priorities.

Once you learn the rules to "play the game" and you know the strategy, you have to be ready to play. If you play by the rules, you're easier to play with. If you're easy to play with and you play "well," you're more likely to be sought out as a team player, and potentially the team leader.

Politics Is a Tool

You also need to be aware that a set of skills needed to operate effectively in any leadership position are skills that many people avoid like the plague. I'm talking about *the skill of playing politics.*

A number of the survey responses I received from women included comments such as, *"Avoid the office politics," "Don't get caught up in the politics. Just do your job."* I could be wrong, but I expect what they meant to say was, *"Don't get caught up in the catty gossip."* If that's what they meant, I agree. However, so often in our attempts to avoid the gossip, we avoid the office politics altogether.

I have trained and consulted with all different types and sizes of organizations for years. One common mistake organizations make in promoting personnel is that the organization will often promote the most *technically* capable individual into the supervisory or managerial spot. Then, the organization gets upset when this new manager has trouble managing former peers and the overall productivity of the department drops. However, what the organization fails to recognize is that the skills needed to effectively manage others are very different from the technical and mechanical skills needed to successfully complete technical calculations or to perform machine operations. How can you expect someone who is technically brilliant at performing tangible calculations or debugging computer programs to have the same success with managing unpredictable people? You wouldn't expect an untrained person to just step in and start programming your computers, now would you?

As an individual changes positions or moves up in a hierarchy, new skills need to be developed. The skills needed to perform at any level are for all intents and purposes "tools." They are the tools that will help get things done. As people move into leadership roles, their toolbox needs to change. Leaders, most obviously, politicians and executives, rely more and more on their networks, relationships, communication skills, and political savvy to get things done. Their ability to be involved with and direct the office politics will determine their success at getting things done.

> *Many people don't like office politics because they don't view it for what it is – a tool.*

I recently worked with a senior management team on its organization's five-year strategic plan. During one of the planning sessions, the discussion turned to a competitor's ability to secure additional financing, because of its political connections. The tone of the comments made it quite clear: My client believed this was an unfair, if not unethical activity by the competitor. I pointed out to the members of the management team that using political connections was what *they* should be doing. They should be using or establishing their political "toolbox" to help get things done.

As leaders, you have to use what tools you need to get the job done. If that means calling on some political connections for help – do it. If it means taking prospective clients out to golf and then dinner a few times – do it. If it means following-up three, four, five or more times – do it. Your job is to get things done, and that often happens out of the office as well as in it.

However, to play politics successfully, you have to accept that playing politics and working your network is your job. Also, be prepared to hear many people in the lower ranks complain about the easy life of the executive staff. *All they do is eat and play golf.* What they don't see or realize is that building a solid network of professional and political connections takes time, practice, and skill. There is a subtle art to creating a comfortable environment for every different client, vendor, or colleague with whom you interact. You have to be able to flex with each one to make the environment comfortable, so each one is comfortable with you. You also have to be aware that others are watching you, just as you're watching them.

Your political skills are your tools. These skills, these tools, allow you to do your job.

Your effectiveness in a position is a countdown of how much you can get done in specified time periods. That's what you're there for; that's how you're measured.

Tip # 3 - Do the Job

In my survey, I asked what bit of advice the respondents would offer a woman in the work world. A consistent theme conveyed in many of the responses was: *Gender is irrelevant. What matters is your ability to do the job.*

As Colleen Stanley, President of Sales Leadership, Inc. put it, "Quit worrying about being a girl. I grew up surrounded by brothers. That particular birth order taught me to be competitive, keep up or get left behind. If you were up to the task, my brothers did not care about your gender."

Your effectiveness in a position is a countdown of how much you can get done in specified time periods. That's what you're there for; that's how you're measured. That's how you become a team player and ultimately – a leader. The Society for Human Resource Management's 2002 Global Leadership Survey noted the most important trait of a leader was:

Performance – getting things done.

You can be a leader and a success today. You don't have to wait for a specific title and position. Position power is useless without the ability to get the job done and without the respect of others. Your effectiveness in any position starts to erode when you lose the respect and confidence of others. True leaders – regardless of position or rank – are a sure thing – a sure thing in getting things done.

You Need to FOCUS

Multitasking is simply a way of life for so many of us. We have become masters of *focusing* on multiple priorities. However, by doing so, we really don't focus well on any one priority. Our focus and our energies are fragmented, so we end up doing everything *adequately* and nothing really *well*.

I have to admit, this is an area where I struggle. Constant multitasking is a habit I've developed over the years. It is one, I believe, many women have developed through the sheer nature of traditional male and female household chores. For instance, mowing the lawn has historically been the man's job. But there's not much else you can do while you're mowing – either pushing a mower or riding a lawn tractor – you keep going back and forth until the job is done. Compare that to cleaning the house – traditionally a woman's responsibility. You can start a load of laundry, load and start the dishwasher, start the self-cleaning oven, pick up clothes and toys as you make piles of things to go to Goodwill, and do all of this while you help the kids learn their ABCs. Many of us are just used to multitasking as a way of life.

However, in your personal and professional worlds, if the job or task is important, it deserves your undivided attention for that moment or for that period of time. Just as you've all heard, "It's not the quantity of time you spend with your kids, but the quality that counts," it's the quality of time you dedicate to your professional or leadership responsibilities that allows you to perform at your best.

> *However, in your personal and professional worlds, if the job or task is important, it deserves your undivided attention for that moment or for that period of time.*

My friend and mentor, Robert Oxley, an expert in sales training and speaking, confirmed this idea as he shared his thoughts on what women do to inhibit their leadership success:

First of all, most men and women don't succeed in business. I don't think it is a gender specific thing. Those men and women who succeed in business do four things that the masses will not do:

#1. They think independently - staying focused on business goals, which always come first.

#2. They have a strong will - staying focused on business goals, which always come first.

#3. They persist until they succeed - staying focused on business goals, which always come first.

#4. They eliminate all distractions - staying focused on business goals, which always come first.

It is my observation that many average women in business tend to be ever distracted. They can't seem to clear their mental or "must do" plate. There are rules and a natural rhythm to conducting business. Nothing kills a sale quicker than violating them.

Second, the law of nature is survival of the fittest. The law of business is to grow and win a return on investment. Just like the hunter gatherers of ol', the person who comes home with the meat wins. But, only for a short while, then it is off again, over and over, getting bigger and better at the game.

Those who succeed in business think differently than those who are in the ranks. They understand that "the numbers" are what count. Nothing gets in the way of making the numbers. Others seem to think it is okay to think and to tell the leaders that they need to get a life, to slow down, and meet in the middle. You'll never get through the glass ceiling, boy or girl, if you can't make the numbers, at any cost.

Show me a woman who has made it to the top and I will be looking at a person who is strong-willed, not distracted easily, focused on one goal at a time, and very independent in her ways.

In business, especially sales, it is the focused will to succeed that is missing from those women and men who don't go from average to GREAT. My education and experiences lead me to understand that it is simply not a "sex" thing. I think it is a "commitment and focus" thing.

True intensity and unwavering focus allows leaders to see what needs to be done and then to pursue it until it is achieved. That intensity is lacking in many women who say they want to be leaders, or who want the top spot. But that focus and intensity will get you there. Ironically, that level of intensity will also earn you the title of "Witch" for being so focused. If you want the top spot, deal with the title. Your critics will then learn to focus on your leadership skills and not your gender.

> *...it is the focused will to succeed that is missing from those women and men who don't go from average to GREAT. My education and experiences lead me to understand that it is simply not a "sex" thing. I think it is a "commitment and focus" thing.*
> Robert Richardson Oxley, CEO - The "from Average to Great" Enterprise

I've seen the truth of this need for focus and intensity time and again with my clients. Those men and women who are able to intently focus on a clear objective – to the exclusion of side distractions – have been able to achieve far more than those who are more easily side-tracked. Why? Because their intense focus is most often accompanied with an intense drive and willingness to get the job done. Other tasks are put aside until *the* task or project is completed. That means things get done quicker, momentum is maintained, and energy levels are higher. My clients with this intense focus have seen solid growth rates; those without, haven't. It's a matter of how bad they want "it."

If you want to get above the glass ceiling, you have to want "it." If you want to be a leadership success in your department, focus on that. Then focus on how to get "it."

This intense focus is not right for many of you, I know. It's too aggressive. You'd never be comfortable or happy operating in that intense mode for very long. So accept that your "less-than-laser-beam focus" is okay too. But then be fair to yourself, and match your vision of leadership success to your level of intensity and focus.

Don't Give Up – Success Doesn't Just Happen

Success is a journey, not a destination.
Fortune cookie insert

We have all heard Murphy's Law:

1. *Nothing is ever as easy as it looks.*
2. *Everything will take longer than you think it will.*
3. *If anything can possibly go wrong, it will.*

Therefore, deal with what goes wrong, and move on. This is difficult for many of us.

We tend to focus on what's not going right, instead of figuring out how to make things right.

Do you remember the *"Life Sucks and Then You Die"* bumper stickers? I've noticed that people with the "Life Sucks" attitude usually limit their own successes. They're not happy with their current professional situation, yet they believe there's nothing else they can do to improve or change it. Maybe they don't know what to do. Maybe they know what to do, but they know it will be difficult, so they back away. Maybe they tried before and failed. Perhaps, they're waiting for someone else to do it for them. Often these people can see others excel with grace, yet they incorrectly assume that those who are successful have somehow been *given* their successes; they didn't have to work for them. These misperceptions inhibit many from seeing opportunities that present themselves.

The road to success is not a straight one with clear directions. There are a lot of twists, turns, detours, and washouts. Being able to target the destination, and then being willing to follow that course, navigate the detours, and take advantage of any shortcuts is how most successful people find success.

They don't wait for someone else to lead them to their success. They cut their own path.

I always found it amusing that the "Life Sucks" bumper stickers were usually on the back bumper of some beat-up old junker that would chug down the interstate at 53 miles per hour. I have yet to see one on the back of a new Jaguar. Also, I have yet to meet someone whom I consider a "successful leader" project a "Life Sucks" attitude. Instead, they face challenges regularly. They expect them. They plan for them. They deal with them. Then, they move on.

> *The road to success is not a straight one with clear directions. There are a lot of twists, turns, detours, and washouts. Being able to target the destination, and then being willing to follow that course, navigate the detours, and take advantage of any shortcuts is how most successful people find success.*

Also, have you noticed that people who have a reputation as a "success" in our culture, rarely believe they are as successful as they should or could be? They believe they could be giving more of themselves or should be taking advantage of other opportunities they have not yet pursued. They are constantly looking to improve themselves or to achieve more. They don't believe they've given their all yet; they haven't done their best yet. Their success is not something that just happened. They worked for it, and they're willing to push themselves to learn and do still more.

> *... a common trait they all share is the self-confidence to make it happen. "It" being whatever it is that they want to accomplish. They all have a high level of self-awareness and resourcefulness that allows them to know what they want and to take the steps necessary to achieve great success.*
> Holli Catchpole - President, SpeakersOffice, Inc.

I'm constantly watching others to see how they do "their thing." I'm readily amazed, that when you really watch others who are "successful," they make what they do look so easy. Yet it comes from years of practice, experience, learning the hard way, and refinement to become more focused and –

yes – confident in who they are and what they do. Identify others you deem "successful leaders." Study them. Watch them. Identify what they do that resonates with others, with their employees, and with their clients. Identify what resonates with you. If something resonates with you, it's more likely to work for you if you apply it in your own arena. Learn from others. Learn for yourself.

Also remember, everyone has had personal and professional challenges. Many of you have had incredible obstacles to overcome. There are many other people out there who would never have accepted the challenges some of you have faced. Be proud of what you have learned, achieved, and accomplished.

There is no quick and easy road to success. But the quickest is to know what it is you want. The truly successful woman is the one who has identified her vision of success and has been able to "see it" in her mind's eye. The vision may not be right for others, but it's right for her. There is no secret to success. There is no secret to becoming a "leader." It takes work and a belief in yourself that you can attain your dream.

*It is our challenges that make us great
and build our character. When you are
in the middle of a trial, just hang tight
and know that you are becoming
stronger and wiser for it. I have gone
through more than my share of tough
times and only looking back now can I
see that I would never have been able to
handle what I am doing today if I had
not weathered those storms.*
Gina Schreck, author of
*Marriage Mechanics, Inside Out Success,
and 10 Steps to Become a Pessimist*

Know when to support. Know when to lead.

Tip # 4 - Don't Be So Willing to Help Out

This insight struck home for me when Christine Oxley shared it with me. I remember thinking to myself, "Oh my gosh! I've done that!"

When she was the only female Property Manager in their office, Christine was told by her former boss, "Don't shift roles."

Christine had been leading a meeting when one of the other property managers stated he couldn't complete his part of a project because he was going on vacation. Christine had replied, "Well then, let me handle it," and took his project file. That's where she messed up. That's why her boss called her into his office. She wasn't managing; she was mothering.

Because she had wanted to get the job done, she had taken on her team member's responsibilities as well as her own. However, when she took on his work and became his "support" person, she had shifted roles from "the leader" to "support staff." If that was done too often, her message to everyone would be that she was the designated support person and not the leader.

To maintain her leadership role, she should have asked this team member, *"What are you planning to do to make sure everything is taken care of before you leave?"* Or, she could have asked, *"Who will be handling these issues while you're away?"* With either question, she would have maintained her status, while continuing to focus herself, this team member, and the entire team, on getting the job done.

Christine further explained:

"You are not their mother, so stop acting as if you are and start acting as their equal."

This comment was made to me in a private meeting, or as my boss called them: "A come to Jesus meeting." He went on to explain that I would never command the respect that I deserved nor would I be treated as a member of the team if I kept getting coffee, helping my male team members with just about everything (i.e., cleaning up their

*offices, redoing their reports, putting to-
gether their meetings, etc.).*

*If I felt trapped to do these "woman things,"
then I should do them poorly; they won't ask
again.*

This tip comes with a caveat, however: You
must support your team members when they
legitimately need it. If you refuse to help
simply because "you're the leader," you just
end up acting like a witch. You've now
failed on several fronts: 1). You didn't
manage your team members and their performance properly; 2). You established, or
re-affirmed, your image as a witch; and 3).
You sent a message to your team that holding the title "leader" is more important than
serving your customers. None of these are
right, fair, or professional.

More importantly, when *not* supporting your
team members puts meeting the client's
needs in jeopardy, you are obligated to support your team however you can.

Your ultimate responsibility is to your customers. However, you have to know when
you need to support your team and when
you need to lead. Your responsibility, even
though you've delegated many tasks, is to

deliver what you've promised. So if a team member drops the ball, and your customers are negatively affected, it's *your* fault. If you're a leader, you're responsible.

Also, remember this tip the next time you're sitting in a meeting and all eyes turn to you to take the meeting minutes, because – you're a girl. Instead of simply sighing, thinking of yourself as a martyr, or lashing out at your team, say something along the lines of, *"I'll take the meeting minutes today. Then, Ted, you take them at our next meeting; Kelly, you the next; and Steve, the next. That way we'll rotate around the table and each of us will have an opportunity to handle this responsibility."* Make it a statement, not a suggestion. Show them how a professional equal would handle the situation. Show them how a leader would handle the situation.

Know when to support. Know when to lead.

Find a Mentor

Don't take advice from unsuccessful people.
Always search out a mentor who is
experienced in the area of knowledge you
wish to learn more about or excel in.
Ed Price – VP, Commercial Banking

A successful grocery wholesaler once told me, *"The bank you use should grow as your business grows. Your banker should always be able to take you to the next level."* That advice holds true for any of your professional advisors as well. You have to be able to depend on your advisors for their expert knowledge and to guide you away from hazards and toward success quicker. If you don't have a mentor – get one. Mentors are unpaid advisors who share their expertise and experience. They've been there, done it, have learned and have been burned; so learn from them. Good mentors are also terribly honest and will tell you when you're screwing up.

I had the opportunity to formally enter into a mentoring program two years ago. My mentor, Robert Oxley, was so generous with his time – our first meeting lasted three hours! That's not normal – so don't expect it. But that first meeting alone was proof to me that just by listening and asking questions, I was learning "insider" secrets that were going to help move my business dramatically forward. Robert has many more years of business experience than I and he specializes in sales – but his insights had direct applicability to my business. He shared his professional contacts, vendors, marketing tactics, business systems, and product development strategies. So many of the things he shared with me seemed minor to him, but to me they were the missing links to some key strategies I had been planning. With his help, my business was propelled forward. Without him, that knowledge and those professional connections would have taken years to develop.

Choose Mentors Well

When I entered the mentoring program, I was very specific in describing the focus and area of expertise I wanted my mentor to have. Also, my mentor needed to have a personality and an intensity level that would challenge me. I was fortunate to have been matched with Robert. I learned a great deal from him and, to this day, consider him my mentor and friend.

It is also important that you give back to your mentor(s) and advisors. As Robert has told me, he believes he learned more through the experience than I did. Because, as he'd mentored me, he was *forced* to review and to re-evaluate why he did what he did. The process also motivated him to improve his own business processes further. We were able to support each other.

However, Robert wasn't and isn't my only advisor. Just as we have different friends in our lives, each one adding her or his own "spice," multiple advisors and mentors can each add to our professional success as well. Besides, we never want to over-tax any one person; it's rude and we'll burn the person out. Also no one advisor is always right. Therefore, we should have different advisors and mentors for different aspects of, and at different times in, our careers. Again, each one will add her or his own "spice."

Be aware that with multiple advisors comes the obvious dilemma of receiving conflicting advice. It's up to you to sift through the advice and determine what's right for you.

Advisors advise. You decide.

To get an attitude, know your stuff.

Tip # 5 - Get an Attitude

Hang out with successful people and you'll become more successful. Good things come to those who make things happen. The other guy isn't responsible for your success, you are!

Holli Catchpole - President,
SpeakersOffice, Inc.

When I say, "Get an Attitude," I don't mean become cocky or arrogant. I mean: *Accept confidence.* Recognize that you should be confident, if you are prepared. There is a big difference between *confidence* and *arrogance*. Confidence is an internal strength that is a result of preparation, knowledge, and a love of solid information. Arrogance is the result of loving yourself more than you love the information. In fact, when you're arrogant, you're often willing to "fudge" the facts just to appear correct. Confident people tend to stand more comfortably on fact.

Over the years, I've trained and coached a number of employees. I particularly remember one young accountant at the U.S. Department of State who was nervous before giving her first briefing. She was panicking, actually. Several inspectors were going to attend, as well as our Director, and other more senior staff. I had seen her preparing for this briefing for days. She was incredibly detail-oriented, knew her data, and had a solid understanding of the ramifications to changes in any one number. Yet she was nervous about addressing the group. Because she would be the youngest person in the room, she worried that the "more senior" staff would not take her seriously.

I remember saying to her, "Kelly, get an attitude." She had looked confused, so I continued, "No one else knows this data like you do. No one in that room has the knowledge you have on this project. It's up to *you* to educate *them*. They need your data so they can make decisions. They'll challenge some of it. But you're the expert on this data; they're not." She started to realize that compared to the people she would be briefing, she *was* the expert. Her head came up higher, her shoulders went back a bit straighter, and she acquired that gut-level confidence, because she *knew* her stuff.

To get an attitude, know your stuff.

> *The will to succeed is important,*
> *but what's more important is the*
> *will to prepare.*
>
> Bobby Knight

Convince – Don't Cave

In my survey, I asked what qualities the respondents most admired in their female co-
workers. The overwhelming response was
*Confidence: the ability to take a stance and
defend a position.* Confidence comes from
assured knowledge that your stance is based
on fact, knowledge, and experienced gut
instinct.

The respondents also stated that this quality,
when missing, irritated them the most. Too
often they had observed women back down,
or defer to a man's position, even though the
woman's position had been stronger. A
woman's unwillingness to firmly stand her
ground – when she had an informed stance
to take – irritated both my female and male
respondents the most. My respondents believe this lack of confidence or low self-
esteem trait, which many women default to,
raises doubt in the minds of those who have
the ability to move women into leadership

positions: *If she is unable to hold her own in this situation, she'll never be able to hold her own against so-and-so who's a barracuda. I can't run that risk. I better go with the guy who has proven he can stand his ground.*

I can't blame them. I'd think the same thing. Seeing is believing.

Christine Oxley shared another leadership tip she learned from her former boss. As Christine told me,

I was in a business meeting. I knew my material since I had spent a great deal of time researching the feasibility and its impact on the company. However, as soon as it was questioned and scoffed at, I backed into "Maybe you're right." My boss exploded after the meeting because I had been right, but my cowering created an environment where it would be very hard to get the rest of the team to believe in my idea and me. He told me, "The strong can smell the weak and they will go for the kill. Act strong even if you are nervous."

So why do so many women back down? Why do they defer to men or more aggressive women? I am not a psychologist or sociologist, but I have noticed most women believe confrontation in the workplace is, well – rude. They are more comfortable walking away from a situation they know is not right, than they are standing their ground and confronting an aggressive co-worker or manager with a contrary view. Why? As so many studies have shown, much of it has to do with genetics, and much has to do with the way we raise girls and boys.

I don't know about you, but I was taught – and I taught my girls – not to interrupt when someone else is speaking. That works well when you're having dinner with your family, but it doesn't work when you're in a meeting debating the merits of Project A over Project B. In a situation like that, if you wait until there's an open and obvious break in the debate to speak, you'll never say a word and the meeting will end with you still waiting to speak. I have sat on a number of boards in which at least one board member hardly ever says a word or introduces an idea. The only time he or she speaks is to vote with the majority. Needless to say, in a very short time, the rest of the board starts to subconsciously ignore that board member because he or she brings nothing new to the table and will side with the majority – so why bother even asking for input? Quiet members are not viewed by the rest of the board as leadership material. They are viewed as followers, because that's what they do. They follow the majority.

The next time you attend a meeting, pay specific attention to the dynamics of the group. If done without overt rudeness, those individuals who aren't afraid to interrupt others, talk over others and stand their ground appear more confident, strong, and capable. Why? Because they were able to communicate their position, then back it up with conviction. They do this even when their idea may be a bit weaker than another person's. An individual's ability to back up her stance and show its merits will win her support, while someone else with a great idea, but who fails to justify its merits and "sell" it to the group, will lose support. Which person would you support? The one who shows conviction and "sells" you on her idea, or the one who backs away from her own idea?

Don't explain. Don't defend.

This sounds as if it is somewhat of a contradiction to the previous section, but it is really a clarifier. As Sheila Murray-Bethel, Ph.D. author of the best selling book, *Making A Difference, 12 Qualities That Make You A Leader,* shared with me:

"Don't explain. Don't defend" is a statement that has served me very well. It means when you have made a decision and are willing to "bet the farm" on it, go with it. You are not required to respond to everyone that challenges you. You don't have to explain yourself; you don't have to defend your views. That does not mean you do not have to compromise, work with others to achieve your goals, or be flexible. It means that just because someone questions you or challenges you – it is not necessary to respond. Keeping your own counsel is often the hardest thing to do. When being attacked for your views or actions, it is easy to feel you have to defend yourself. You do not. Stand tall and as they say "hang tough." Better to go down with pride than win having given up all your principles or values.

Knowing when and how to stand your ground, as well as when and how much to clarify your position is critical. Don't explain and justify every decision you make. As a leader, you don't have to. You need to get things done. You can explain and justify if there is a real sense of confusion, but to do so regularly presents an image that you can't make decisions by yourself; you have to run them by others first, and that's not a leadership trait. You have to be willing to stand your ground, defend your stance when necessary, and keep moving forward.

Know your stuff. Get an attitude. Project confidence. Become a leader.

> *Don't explain and justify every decision you make. As a leader, you don't have to.*

Mix Grace with Power

Many of my survey respondents also stated that those women they most admired were able to balance the challenges of their work worlds (personnel, technology, budgets, strategy, etc.) with grace.

Grace is a beautiful word that makes one think of courtesy, elegance, and an ability to project oneself as if each challenge were an opportunity. Grace in others is projected by their skill in not carrying their overwhelming responsibilities around on their sleeves as burdens, but rather as opportunities. In turn, they also treat those around them, their supporters and their opponents, with the same degree of professionalism. However, when it is time to hold another accountable for not doing his or her job, these graceful professionals hold others accountable in a firm, direct, and fair way.

> *Grace is a beautiful word that evokes courtesy, elegance, and an ability to project oneself as if each challenge were an opportunity.*

Patti Anfang, Senior Buyer, Bruno Independent Living Aids, Inc., provided this description of a confident, graceful co-worker:

Judy has been through adversity and staggering personal loss. But to meet her one would never know. She's had tough times but works through them and reaches "Acceptance." Judy is an employer's best friend or its worst nightmare. I say that because she is the eternal optimist. She has

eyes that sparkle with joy and mischief. Her
laugh is easy and frequent. She loves to
work and is a very competitive sales person.
She is a wonderful team player who gives
positive reinforcement to all around her
with ease (if deserved). However, Judy be-
comes management's worst nightmare when
it fails to meet its Mission Statement. When
common sense fails to rule and the com-
pany's integrity is compromised, Judy
shares her concerns. But, not before she
has every duck in a row to prove her point.
She is very detail-orientated and uses that
skill to map a return to a "fair" game plan.

I know this is starting to sound impossible.
How can you be focused, intense, willing to
take risks, get the job done, and do it all
with grace and ease? You can't. You can't
until you get it clear in your mind what your
responsibilities are at work and what they
are in all of the other areas of your life.

When you're at work, your job is to do the
job. Get things done. It's not to make
friends, mother the staff, or have everyone
like you. Your job is to do the job. So
while you're fulfilling your role at work,
that's where your focus needs to be. You
don't have to be cold and abrupt to be fo-

cused. Too often those attributes come as a packaged deal.

I received many wonderful stories that described how many women my contributors respected were fair, firm, professional, and effective. A person who behaves in the same manner with everyone, regardless of position, and respects the input and ideas of others, is a professional. Male and female, graceful persons accept the responsibilities and problems posed each day with an open mindset, a *can-do* attitude, and a willingness to fight for what is right. They fulfill their jobs gracefully.

Mix power and grace. It can happen. It does happen. It's just not easy.

Confidence is an internal strength that is a result of preparation, knowledge, and a love of solid information. Arrogance is the result of loving yourself more than you love the information.

Be comfortable with the fact that not everyone will like you, at work, in your neighborhood, and in your community activities; they never will.

Tip # 6 - Not Everyone Will Like You

*The first lesson I learned as a leader was
that I must be willing to let people
be mad at me.*
Bobbi Silten, President, Dockers® Brand, U.S.,
Levi Strauss & Co.

The most important *leadership* lesson I ever
learned from my dad – I learned at his funeral.

My dad died of colon cancer in 1992. Four
days before he died, I had the opportunity to
spend several hours alone with him. During
that time, he shared stories of his childhood
and other good and bad times in his life. He
also shared something that I had never
known. Each fall, Dad would personally
drive excess clothing and goods from the St.
Vincent de Paul store in my hometown in
Wisconsin to an Indian reservation in South
Dakota. The people on the reservation
would then tear up the clothing, weave the
cloth into rugs and other products, and sell

their work. In sharing this story, Dad described how the manager from a neighboring store would not readily cooperate in providing excess clothing or contribute money for gas. This man's behavior frustrated my father. This man stonewalled my dad every year because he didn't understand how the contribution of excess clothing would help more than a direct infusion of cash. Dad wanted to help the people on the reservation produce their own products and make their own money, not simply hand money to them. He believed it would help them maintain their dignity, creativity, and self-reliance.

At Dad's funeral, a man approached me to convey his condolences (I'd assumed). He shook my hand and introduced himself. His name meant nothing, until he said where he worked. Then it hit me. *This* was the man my dad had talked about just four days before! After introducing himself the man said, "You know, I never liked your dad." *(I tried my best not to interrupt him to ask if he'd ever heard of Funeral Etiquette 101 – i.e., Don't insult the deceased.)* Then he continued, "But he was a good businessman. He was a leader."

Those words hit home. This man's need to convey his respect for my dad overrode his personal dislike of my dad.

His comment changed my life and how I viewed my professional responsibilities. I no longer felt the need to please everyone or have everyone like me. Because my dad had stayed true to his beliefs, he had earned this man's respect.

That was when I finally realized, that just as I had never liked everyone in school, not everyone had liked me. At work, I didn't like everyone, so why should I care if everyone liked me? I didn't want to be friends with all of the people at work. I simply wanted to work well with them. Before that night, I had run myself ragged trying to please everyone. I had tried to keep them happy and had tried to make sure they were happy with me. No more.

I finally realized I could now focus on doing what I needed to do to the best of my ability and could forget the rest. Not everyone would like me no matter what I did, because not everyone would share my views. All I could do was do what I believed was right and potentially earn the respect of others. Regardless, I'd be comfortable with myself.

Be comfortable with the fact that not everyone will like you, at work, in your neighborhood, and in your community activities; they never will. Jesus, Gandhi, and Mother Teresa weren't liked by everyone. So how can you and I possibly expect to attain 100% adoration? If we try to achieve that, we'll bend and flex so much no one will know what we stand for – including ourselves.

> *Never compromise your standards just to please someone else. I don't mean not to compromise to reach a solution, but always maintain your moral, business, and personal standards.*
> Joseph Colucci,
> Human Resources Consultant

Take a Risk – Take a Stance

Think of three to five individuals you consider successful leaders. Now for each, identify what event, situation, or development you associate with each.

If you notice, each leader is linked to a major, life-changing, or difficult situation.

That's why they're thought of as leaders. They guided others through uncertain and difficult times. These events weren't normal or life-as-usual situations. Life-as-usual doesn't require anyone to lead it. In that environment, people can operate on autopilot.

Therefore, to lead others, don't be afraid to take a risk and take a position that others will not like. If you do, many will not like you. Some may even come to hate you because of your position. Does the thought of that make you want to run? It will for many, because many people don't want to cause any waves. But if you want to be a leader, you've got to be willing to cause some tidal waves every now and then! How will you ever break through the glass ceiling if you don't create waves? That's how things get done. That's how monumental changes take place in organizations. That's how careers are propelled forward. That's how lives change.

Besides, people who are willing to take a position are, frankly, more interesting. Agree with them or not, you know where they stand. They tug at your emotions: excitement, anger, anticipation, and fear. They cause you to think of alternative views and to grow intellectually.

> *But if you want to be a leader, you've got to be willing to cause some tidal waves every now and then! How will you ever break through the glass ceiling if you don't create waves? That's how things get done.*

Reflect on some of the individuals you've heard about in the news lately or who are regular guests on the radio or television news shows. They're invited to participate because they're willing to express their opinions. They're willing to say things that will excite some; dismay others. Controversy and opinions are what sell in the media. You're never going to please everyone, but at least you can be comfortable and honest expressing your views professionally and clearly.

Take a risk and take a stance by being willing to take personal responsibility. The willingness to state a contrary view, "take a hit," or be blamed for something is huge. Take the hit. Then clarify or resolve the issue. That takes real leadership courage and skill.

> *Besides, people who are willing to take
> a position are, frankly,
> more interesting.*

As You Move Up, You Will Change

As the saying goes, *"You are the average of the five people you associate with most."* Therefore, as you move up in an organization and take on more and more challenging roles, you by default interact more and more often with people with a different mindset and different behavior patterns than those with whom you previously interacted. Be ready for subtle and not-so-subtle changes to take place in your behavior. Be ready for your friends to criticize or comment on those changes as well.

A new section manager had a hard time accepting this fact as he was moving up in the company. We had just completed a training session on personality and leadership styles when Randy approached me. He was frustrated with his self-assessment results. He didn't want to be the person described in his assessment results. He wanted to be "the fun one." Instead, Randy's results were indicating that he was more focused, goal-oriented, and driven than he'd realized. However, in the prior day's training, his production team had taken similar self-assessments and had quickly identified Randy as no longer "fun"; he was now the "Task-master." Since he'd gotten that last promotion, he'd changed.

If you really want a leadership spot, don't expect to make many friends in the workplace or to keep the same relationships with the friends you currently have. As people move up in the hierarchy of an organization, they take on more and more responsibilities and need to make decisions quicker and quicker. The sheer magnitude of the issues they have to deal with on an hourly, much less daily, basis, prohibit them from being able to project the same caring, nurturing characteristics they readily and regularly shared before. It's not that they don't care anymore. It's just that they have numerous other issues weighing on them so they can't become too absorbed with one personnel issue that has minimal potential impact on their overall range of responsibilities. And that's where their focus is – and rightly so.

Because of this shift and growth in responsibilities, I hear those on the front lines say things such as, "She's too good for us now. She used to sit with us during breaks and talk, but she doesn't anymore. This promotion has gone to her head." You know what? They're right. The promotion did go to her head. If this is how she now behaves, she now understands her increased responsibilities don't allow time for her to talk with her former colleagues as much as she used to. She has more things to handle in the same limited number of hours each day. Besides, many of the new leadership issues she has to address aren't topics open for discussion with her former peers. They are topics to be discussed with her new peers or with her advisors outside the company.

I recently started working with a financial institution. In one of our conversations, the CEO relayed several problems she was encountering with one of her senior staff members. The CEO also stated that she had shared these frustrations with other members of the senior staff. Not good. By doing this, she was creating a we/they environment within the company and the employees would soon sense that sides were forming. I told her, "As CEO, you have no peers in this organization. No one can relate to your level of responsibility or to the issues you have to address. You have no 'dumping' ground here. You have no friends here like your staff does. Talk to your mentor. Talk to your advisors. Talk to your professional peers outside this organization. Just don't 'dump' on your staff."

You have to remember what your position is and what your responsibilities are. If you do your job well, you will change.

As You Move Up, Friends Will Change

A woman who had received a promotion once asked me how she should deal with her friends who were starting to complain about her more hectic work schedule. They couldn't as easily get together at night or on the weekends to hang out. Her friends were getting angry and frustrated with her. She said she felt as if she had to choose between her friends and her job. I told her that her true friends would be there whenever she really needed them, and she'd be there when they really needed her. True friends will want you to fulfill your professional dreams and goals. They'll help you however they can. They'll be willing to rearrange their schedules to be conducive with yours. You'll do the same for them. Some of your friends won't understand that your leadership opportunities are a challenge, as well as an opportunity for you to pursue your dreams. These friends may not be long-term friends. They're good people, but you *may* grow away from them as you grow professionally.

Life changes. You will change. Friends will change.

*Get to the point. Tell them what they
need to know so they can
keep moving forward.*

Tip # 7 - Get to the Point

Communicate more precisely and more powerfully. Be blunt when necessary, but get to the point.

It is often said that women have a natural advantage over men in that we are genetically wired to be better listeners. Wonderful, but then when we respond to a comment or question, we tend to provide too much background information in our response. We want to make sure everyone is on the same wavelength before moving ahead, so we go into great detail and history to properly set the stage.

Men don't view this setting-the-stage information as necessary, but rather as a waste of time. Because of this, we lose points and credibility with them. Men in general have a "get it done" mentality. For them, don't waste time talking about the obvious. Just give them your direct response first. Then if necessary, provide your thoughts on how you got there.

To get a sense of this "Get to the Point" idea, listen to some call-in talk radio programs. The really good interviewers, male and female, quickly interrupt a caller if the caller is not answering the interviewer's question directly, is giving background information before she answers the question, or answers the question with a question. The point is: answer the question; provide the information requested. Provide your proposed solution first. Then if necessary, provide your logic in arriving at that point. It's similar to the stereotypical male preference not to ask directions: *Don't tell me how to get there. Just get me there. If I'm really lost – and it's obvious – then I'll ask for directions.*

...don't waste time talking about the obvious. Just give them your direct response first. Then if necessary, provide your thoughts on how you got there.

In the workplace the thought process is: Don't tell me how you reached your conclusion – just reach it. If I can't determine how you came to that conclusion, I'll ask. Otherwise, you're wasting my time by telling me something I've already figured out for myself.

One of the advisory boards I sat on years ago had oversight of a dynamic organization. The director was young and very energetic, worked long hours and turned the organization around. We all appreciated the 14 to 16 hour days she worked, but we didn't need to hear how much time she had put into making it happen at each meeting. Instead of simply listing the accomplishments for the prior month and the planned initiatives for the coming period, she would spend more time talking about how much she had worked than on what had been accomplished, or what we really needed to know.

Many people like to have others experience their pain with them and acknowledge their hard work. Some people seem to thrive on reliving their misery. However, on this board, we all either owned our own businesses or were in senior management positions. Working 14 to 16 hour days was the norm for us. The director's long hours were not surprising. At that time, the organization needed that amount of time from her, and she had known that going into the position. Therefore, her comments often sounded whiny.

As a professional, as a leader, you're expected to work hard. Most jobs require that you work hard. But we all work hard. What's really going to impress us is: *What did you accomplish? If you've accomplished what we've planned – wonderful. That's what we wanted. Thanks for doing a great job. We're making solid progress. However, if you're accomplishing more than we planned, now it's time to take notice, to talk it up more, and to commend you on your hard work and accomplishments.*

Get to the point. Tell others what they need to know so they can keep moving forward.

Learn the Lingo

Every organization – whether it's a corporation, not-for-profit, government agency, or sports team – has its own culture, its own rules, its own way of doing things, and its own jargon. That's normal and natural. It's no different than my family having its own culture, rules, ways of doing things, and jargon. Because it's natural for groups of people to develop their own cultures, expect organizations staffed by a good number of men to have a culture and language that is more "manly" – possibly more sports oriented – and less emotionally charged, than one staffed predominantly by women.

Just as you'd have to learn to fit into my family's ways of doing things if you were to stay with us for an extended visit, you have to learn to fit into the culture of wherever you work. The quickest way to alienate yourself from your colleagues is to walk in the front door and demand that they change the rules they've been happily working with for years, because you're a woman and you're working with them now. I know how I'd feel if that happened in my office: I'd tell you to take a hike. *Who the heck do you think you are walking in here and demanding that what has been working very smoothly and effectively for years be changed just because of what you are – not what you know?*

What is as equally irritating is if you stand apart and isolate yourself from the established group because you don't like the culture. You don't like the culture? Fine. Then leave. Work someplace else.

> *You don't like the culture? Fine.*
> *Then leave. Work someplace else.*

That comment probably made some of you angry and you might be saying, "But if there's something wrong and I don't take a stand, it will never change!" You're right – *if* the culture that is established is violating some moral or legal code such as allowing sexually harassing behaviors. Then you have an obligation to do something about formally changing the culture. However, if the culture is just simply a bit more "manly" than you'd like (i.e., your colleagues talk about football and golf more than about their kids), get over it. There's nothing discriminatory about that. It's just the organization's culture. So if you want to work and thrive in that organization, learn to become a part of the culture. One way several of my contributors advised to help become a part of the culture was: *Learn to play golf.*

Learn to play or become knowledgeable about golf, football, car racing, soccer or whatever *the* favored sport or activity is in your organization. The key is to understand the game or activity so you can talk about it with others. This allows you to expand your network of connections. Since golf seems to be the favored sport by those who responded to my survey, that's what I'll focus on here.

We're all well aware that more deals are made on the golf greens than in many sales calls. For those who don't play golf it seems unfair. Well, remember the adage: *When in Rome...*? If success is achieved more quickly on the greens than elsewhere in your professional world, learn the game. Now don't panic. You don't have to become a really good player. I worked at a country club while in college and was amazed at how bad some of the members were. In most cases, your skill level isn't what's important. What is important is: *Can you spend four hours on the course comfortably with your colleagues and clients? Do you have a good time together? Can you build a comfortable relationship with them?*

By learning the sport, you're able to get people out on the course with you. That's where relationship building occurs. That's where you build your political and professional network.

The important thing is how you *play*. You can't be a jerk. I've played in tournaments and have heard comments such as, *"I'll never do business with that guy. You should've seen the fit he threw when he sliced on 12."* How do you deal with a sliced shot? How serious are you? How much do you whine when you get hot and tired? Do you have a killer mentality on the course? Do you laugh and joke around the entire time? How you *play* tells others about you and may give them some insight into how you work.

You have to be able to know at least enough about the game and its key players to have solid conversations with others about the sport. You want other men and women to have relaxed conversations with you on something other than work. Sports unify people quickly. Because the goal in any sporting event is clear to everyone involved, sports unify those who participate and watch. Also, the strategy formulation in every sport is fascinating once you start studying the sport. There is an obvious strategy to football. But there are also unique strategies used in golf, car racing, horse racing, and all other sports as well. In addition, the strategy and skill required to be good at any sport earns respect for those who are good.   An appreciation of those skills and the strategies needed to play helps you bond with others who appreciate them as well.

> *Learn to play golf. A lot of business happens on the golf course. Play a lot of golf with other women. More happens on the golf course than men want to admit. Playing golf frequently with women makes men wonder what power transactions happened that they missed. Let them sweat a bit. They'll be brought up to speed later.*
> Deirdre Morgan,
> Friend

But what if you don't like sports and prefer crafts? What if you don't want to have to think and form strategies when you relax? Fine. Keep doing your crafts. That's *your* time, and we all need our down time. But you could occasionally watch sporting events while you do your crafts. You could skim the headlines on the sports page or just pay attention to the sports reports on the radio as you drive to work. It doesn't take much to pick up the basics.

Condoleeza Rice, Ph.D. and U.S. National Security Advisor, grew up competing at the national level in figure skating. She also loves football. Given her position as U.S. National Security Advisor, which sport do you think she's able to connect with her colleagues on – figure skating or football? I'm comfortable in saying I don't think she hides the fact that she was a competitive figure skater. That's impressive. But it's easier to picture her conversing regularly with the President and the Secretary of Defense about football than about figure skating.

Stretch yourself to learn a bit about sports. Just being able to chat briefly about the sports that others in the office thrive on will help you fit in. It appears very "girly" not to know about *any* sport. Make it easy for others to interact with you.

Learn their game. Learn their lingo.

*Don't play, "I want to act like a girl
now, but I want to be treated like a
professional equal later."*

Tip # 8 - Stop the "Girly" Behaviors

As I said before, I'm not suggesting you should not be proud you're a woman. I'm saying you *should* be proud you're a woman. Therefore, don't demean yourself by doing or saying things that are self-defeating or demeaning. Don't do things that present you as a ditz or overly "girly."

Be Consistent

Don't play, *"I want to act like a girl now, but I want to be treated like a professional equal later."*

To be consistent, we have to stop playing both sides of the game – intentionally or unintentionally. One of my male contributors, Terry McGee, P.E., Chief Engineer, shared:
Rely on your skills, not your gender. All too often I see women who want to play both

sides of the gender issue, depending upon which side happens to best suit their needs at that moment. That is, "Treat me differently because I'm a woman," and "Don't treat me differently because I'm a woman." I quickly lose respect for such individuals. Good skills rise to the top whether you're a man or woman.

Terry's comments highlight the fact that guys *do* pick up on the mixed signals. They can tell when we're behaving like girls instead of adult professionals. But we can pick up when they're acting like a bunch of boys too. So let's be fair. If we want to be treated like professionals, we need to behave as such. Be consistent.

Also, we don't need to work harder than anyone else just to prove ourselves. We just need to focus on our responsibilities and remember we have a position to fill and a job to do – just as the men do.

Do the job. Be fair. Be consistent.

Don't Take This Personally, But...

Men seem clearer on this than many women: work is work; personal life is personal.

In the professional world, an ability to separate your personal likes and dislikes from your professional responsibilities is crucial. The clarity with which some men are able to separate work issues from personal feelings became very clear to me when I worked with a group of county highway department workers a few years ago.

I had been asked to provide them with mandatory teambuilding training, because they were constantly bickering and "ripping" on each other to the point of near blows. This was not my typical training subject matter, nor was it my typical type of training participant, but my client told me, "No one else will do it." (Talk about a no-win situation.) Because my client was in a bind, I took the project.

I had heard the guys were ready to rip me apart because they thought I would make them participate in some "touchy-feely" training. Knowing they'd be dreading the training, I walked into the room and told them all to stand up. Once they did, I looked at them and said, "Now, let's have one big group hug." They looked at me in horror. I couldn't control my facial expressions for long and laughed with them as they, one by one, realized I was joking. That was the icebreaker they needed to allow me to say, "Okay, what's going on that you guys need *mandatory team building training*?" With a little more prodding, they started sharing their colorful but honest thoughts. They also started ripping on each other as they always apparently did.

We worked through some pretty heated interactions. Then at break, I heard one of the more vocal and combative men say to his victim, "Are we still going hunting this weekend?" I was shocked! These two guys were actually planning to go into the woods together – with guns! Then it dawned on me: To them – work is work; personal life is personal. Just because they didn't like working together didn't mean they wouldn't hunt together.

When we reconvened, we worked through their concerns and ended with some specific changes that needed to take place with them and with their managers. They needed to work together more effectively – and safely – period. Personal likes and dislikes had to be isolated from professional responsibilities. They had jobs to do.

I have known many women who can handle this separation beautifully too. However, I've seen many people in client organizations who will do whatever it takes *not* to have to work or socialize with people they don't like. They'll avoid them like the plague. A personal dislike in their professional or personal world carries over into every other world. To them it's personal regardless of where it takes place. Too often it impacts their ability to maintain their professionalism.

> Work is work; personal life is personal.

Control Your Emotions

Lead with your heart and manage with your head. Don't confuse the two roles; it won't work in reverse.
Jim Cathcart, author of *The Eight Competencies of Relationship Selling*

As Susanne Cardella noted earlier in her Rules of Business, "Rule #1 - No emotions allowed (except anger). Men punch walls out of frustration, women cry. Crying is taboo because men don't do it."

Yes, women cry more easily than men. Crying is how we women deal with emotional extremes – anger, joy, fear, etc. However, when tears start to roll in the professional arena, our credibility and leadership capabilities fall into question. Guys just don't cry as easily, and therefore, they don't understand it or like it when we do. It simply comes across as "girly." It shows a blatant shift from "leader" to "girl."

One of my contributors shared advice she had been given by a former manager. Upon seeing her get "wet eyes" during a confrontation in a senior staff meeting, he had told her, *"Get stronger shoulders if you plan to make it in senior management."*

Keep in mind: You have a job to do and responsibilities to complete instead of personal attacks to return. You'll be less emotionally charged and the tears will be less likely to flow if you keep your responsibilities – instead of your personal feelings – in the forefront.

However, we do need to show some emotion. That's how we connect with our clients and employees. We just have to control our emotional highs and lows. This can be pretty tough because when we're put in leadership positions, we get excited and nervous. Our emotions and desires to do the job well can get out of check. As a result, we may overcompensate in our attempts to be a professional and to fulfill our leadership responsibilities. We, at times, become "The Control-Bitch," as one of my respondents defined the behavior.

There is a big difference between leadership skills and controlling skills. Leaders are *in control*, but they're not *controlling*. Controlling individuals appear self-conscious, unsure, paranoid, and tend to micro-manage. They're basically out of control, while individuals who are in control appear self-assured, confident, aware, and in control. Again, remember you have a job to do and responsibilities to fulfill.

> *Control your emotions or they*
> *will control you.*
> Chinese Adage

It's NOT Your Prerogative

Don't demean yourself with language such as, "I'm a woman. It's my prerogative to change my mind if I want." If we women say things like that, we sound like ditzes. We're basically saying we didn't think when we made the decision the first time, so we're going to try something different now.

Men change their minds too, but they don't rationalize it by saying, "It's a man's prerogative." They rationalize it with some change in gut instinct, a changed situation, or new information. Women have gut instincts just as men do. Our gut instincts and intuition are based upon our past experiences. We can sense when something's dangerous, wrong, or just right – usually because we've had an experience or two like that before.

Therefore, give yourself credit. If it's appropriate to change your mind, do it. However, credit your decision on your trusted gut instinct, a changed situation, or new information; not your hormones.

Take and Give Credit

I have seen many women become embarrassed when complimented and either joke away the compliment or sarcastically boast about their "brilliance" instead of simply accepting the compliment gracefully.

If you joke away or boast away a compliment, the person giving the compliment has to spend more time reiterating to you the value of what you did – so drop it. You don't need to justify or explain that what you did was simple or that it was difficult. Just thank the individual for appreciating what you did. It shows them that you can accept others' recognition of your efforts.

Let them give you their compliments when deserved. Accept them with grace. Accept them like a pro.

Watch Out for the Office "Frou-Frous"

Does your office or work area look like a professional's or does it look like knick-knack heaven?

Several years ago, I met with a woman who was the manager of a regional insurance office. When I walked into her office all I could see were black and white blotches. Her office was decorated in a Holstein cow motif! The office was full of cows. There were stuffed cows, cow caricatures, cow mugs, and cow figurines on every bookshelf and in every corner. Cow pictures covered the walls. There were cows everywhere! It would have been less distracting had I been meeting with the owner of a dairy, or with the Director of the National Association of Holstein Lovers, but I wasn't.

I have to admit, her choice of office décor did cause me to question her capabilities as an insurance professional. Her office's "theme" did not match or support her profession. It was a complete departure. Her office seemed to scream that her real love and interest was Holsteins – not insurance.

Your work area needs to reflect your personality but you also want it to project the right image. If your office is overflowing with flowers, potpourri, and pictures of puppies, you're sending others signals about your personality. Others will form opinions of you, your confidence, your abilities, and your professionalism by your space.

Look at your office or work area. What message are you sending? What message do you want to send? Let your work area reflect your personality, but let it highlight your professional side.

*Don't be ignorant of your family's
finances. Don't act like a girl and
run from money management.*

Tip # 9 - Understand Money

Contrary to what some people say, you can't live on love; you need money. You don't necessarily need a lot. You just need enough to meet your needs and hopefully, live in the style you want. However, if you regularly spend more than you earn, you have problems. Not only do you *not* have control over your personal finances, but you also run the risk of not being able to control your organization's finances. You won't be viewed as leadership material unless you can demonstrate a good, basic understanding of money.

Let's face it, organizations exist to make money. We all work to make money. If we can't manage it, we can't do our jobs and therefore, we're not going to last long. If we can't manage it in our personal lives, we're going to live with constant financial worries.

Faith Popcorn and other market trend predictors have been saying it for years: The woman's market is becoming the dominant target consumer market.

According to data presented in February 2002 by the Business Women's Network:

- Women spend $3.3 trillion per year on consumer purchases.
- Women purchase 81% of all products and services, both business and consumer, and thereby impact trillions of dollars of sales.
- Women handle 75% of all household finances; 53% of all family investment decisions are made by women.
- Women make 81% of all retail purchases and buy 82% of all groceries.
- Women in business will invest $44.5 billion in high technology office products this year and billions more for office supplies.
- Women comprise 53% of all purchasing agents in corporations.

With this kind of economic and financial power, why do so many women run from understanding money and the numbers?

Well, a number of people, women and men, are just not good with numbers and money – period. And they usually know it.

However, as I said before, your responsibility at work is to get the job done. Often that includes managing some type of budget. Your ability to control that budget is one of the most important indicators of your ultimate leadership ability. How you handle money and how you talk about money convey strong messages to others about your leadership potential.

Who would you choose to take over Project X with a $2-million-dollar budget? Tina, who has completed every project on time, has a loyal staff, has experience with Project X-type work, and makes comments such as, "I don't like dealing with money," or Beth, who also has completed every project on time, has a loyal staff, has *less* experience with Project X-type work, but makes comments such as, "We've controlled worse budgets before. We can do it again." I'd feel more confident in giving Beth the nod.

Being able to control money is being able to control the life-blood of your organization, department, or project. I've seen business owners hand over shoe-boxes filled with receipts to their accountants "to handle" each month. I've heard horror stories of business owners tracking checks by rounding the numbers up or down because the numbers were easier to track that way! That's downright frightening.

As one of my MBA professors used to say: "Cash is King." If you don't have money, you can't operate. Control the money and you can better control the business. But, you can't control your money until you understand it.

Do Not Depend on a Man for Money

"Oh I can't handle money. I let my husband handle all of that. If I did, I'd spend everything we have!" I cringe whenever I hear a woman say something like that. What a "girly" attitude to have! That may have been an acceptable mindset in the 1950's, but that's a terribly vulnerable mindset to put yourself in now.

Women need to plan for and invest in their own financial and retirement futures. With the national divorce rate close to 50%, the risk of being widowed or otherwise losing a partner, and with the increasing numbers of women choosing to stay single longer or never marrying, women need to understand and manage money wisely. None of us wants to be in a situation in which, if we suddenly find ourselves alone, we don't know what to do with or about money. We don't need to be the primary breadwinners nor do we need to be expert financial analysts. But, at a bare minimum, we need to understand how to make money, how to control expenses, how to invest in wise purchases, and how to invest for our futures.

When a woman places her complete financial understanding and trust in her mate, she puts herself in a vulnerable position. If they split or her mate dies, the adult woman now has a limited ability to take care of herself. Fact is fact; you need money to live. If that base resource is not in your control, just about every other aspect of your life will be negatively impacted. You don't need to be wealthy, but you need to have enough money to live. If you don't know how to bring in and manage enough money to support yourself and anyone else you're responsible for supporting, you've set yourself up for a very stressful life. Be a partner in your personal *and* financial relationships.

Now I'm not saying your spouse or mate can't be the primary earner in your family. However, if your mate is the primary earner, you still need to understand your family's finances and be involved in managing the money. Don't be ignorant of your family's finances. Don't act like a girl and run from money management.

"Don't depend on any man, not your husband, not your father, not your brother, not your uncle. You have to go to school and study and make a living for yourself so if you are ever not happy in a situation you can walk away and make your life better."

Those were words from my father and have helped me because I did study hard and have made myself self-sufficient. If I'm not happy in a situation, whether it be with a man or in a job, I know that the hard work I have endured to get to where I am allows me to search for other opportunities. I never have to stay in one place because of money.
Susana Ramirez, CPA

Shop 'Til You Drop

I've noticed over the years, that some women become shop-aholics when they're not happy with some core component of their lives. When their personal relationships are a mess, they are over their "ideal weight," their jobs are shaky, or they face some other "issues," they resort to shopping for an escape. *Maybe a new pair of shoes or new outfit will make it all better?* However, the charges they ring up on their credit cards just add to their mess even more.

On the other hand, I've noticed that women who are pretty comfortable in their own skin don't seem to shop that much. They shop, but it's not an escape for them. They shop because it's necessary, and they usually have the financial resources to handle their expenses comfortably.

A woman I used to work with was going through a rough period with her boyfriend. She asked me to go shopping with her and we did. We both ended up making some purchases, then stopped back at her house to drop off her packages. As she opened her closet to put some of her new items away, she showed me clothes and shoes still in their original packages, with their original sales tags attached. She'd never worn them. She'd just shopped to make herself feel better! I was stunned. Something was out of control here.

At work, watch comments such as, *"I'm going shopping to feel better."* That's a "girly" thing – and it sounds wasteful. If I were your manager, that type of comment would make me wonder what you might do with the company budget – *just to feel better.* Repressing emotions by spending money creates a vicious cycle of money problems and emotional worries. Personally and professionally, it's self-defeating and dangerous.

Control your emotions. Control your finances. Control yourself and you're better able to do the job.

Know What You're Worth

The facts are out there, women still earn less than their male counterparts. Even though the trend is changing, according to a March 2002 Census Report, women are still less likely than men to reach the highest salary brackets. Almost 16% of men age 15 and older who worked full-time in 2001, earned at least $75,000, while only 6% of women in the same age category did so. About 20% of men earned $50,000 to $75,000, compared with 12% of women.

One way to combat this and to be viewed as a more viable professional equal is to better negotiate your compensation, wages, and fees.

A couple key bits of advice need to be itemized here. They may appear elementary, but most of us don't follow them. As a result, we end up earning less than what we should be earning.

1. **Research what your position is worth in the marketplace.** Based upon your experience, skills, education, and accomplishments, what are you worth? You have to know what your realistic target compensation rate should be. Most of you don't have a clue what that is. You just know what you'd like to earn. Compared to the true market rate, you may be high; you may be low. You're guessing.

    You don't want to overshoot, and you certainly don't want to sell yourself short. You've got to know what the right range is. Then if you like it – great. However, if you don't like the compensation rate because it's too low, you're prepared and won't mistakenly think you're being offered less because you're female. Instead, you'll know – that's the position's value.

You probably won't be able to find out *exactly* what others are making who have been in or who are presently in comparable jobs, but you can get a ballpark figure. Search the Internet for this data. Sites such as:

- *www.hotjobs.com*
- *www.salary.com*
- *www.monster.com*

include tools and search features for this information. Contact your local chapter of the Society for Human Resource Management. Many chapters prepare an annual wage survey to gauge the wages in their respective areas. You may be able to buy one of the surveys from the local chapter. Go to *www.shrm.org* to find your local chapter.

Once you identify what your salary range should be, realize that the prospective employer is not going to offer you the salary at the top end of the scale – unless you are THE expert in the industry. Most people aren't. So you have to be ready to anticipate that, at best, they're going to offer you something in the middle to lower-end of the salary range. You now have to identify what realistic salary you'd be happy receiving.

2. **Identify your bare minimum package.** To ensure you don't accept something that will not work for you after the initial honeymoon period, you have to identify what your bare minimum salary and package deal would be. What is the minimum salary you need to earn? Which benefits are a *must*, and which would just be nice to have? What are you willing to give up? Which benefits do you miss? Which benefits do you actively utilize? Which ones are rather useless? You have to determine these tangible and intangible values yourself. This allows you to establish your "floor" for negotiating. Anything less than the "floor" offer, constitutes a *"No"* from you, and you walk away. Sample benefits include fully or partially-paid medical insurance, 401(k) and other retirement

plans, stock options, extra vacation days, day care, elder care, health or country club memberships, company cars, cell phones, internet connections for your house (to allow work from home), newspapers and trade subscriptions delivered to your house, relocation costs, and position title enhancements.

Also, you'll need to determine which benefits would help position you for a future promotion or move. If the company can't offer you more money, seek a title change. That alone can carry a lot of credibility on your resume when you're seeking a promotion or have to look for work elsewhere: once a Vice President, always a Vice President. It doesn't matter if you were the Vice President of a firm with only two employees, that was your title.

3.   **Identify your dream package.** Once you've identified your minimum salary and benefits package, identify what you'd love to receive: your dream deal. This exercise allows you to identify your "ceiling." Anything offered between your

floor and ceiling is worthy of reviewing. Anything offered below the floor is a walk-away. Anything over the ceiling needs to be reviewed for any hidden catches. You can "Whoo-hoo!" to yourself, but you need to control your emotions and identify the unspoken expectations of the employer (i.e., 75% travel, weekend shifts, etc.) The dream packages often hold them. You can celebrate after the deal is sealed.

4.   **Negotiate the package**. Once you have identified your minimum and maximum (i.e., your floor and ceiling), you're ready to start the negotiation process. However, to do this effectively, you've got to be prepared. Do your homework and research now. Talk to colleagues, search the Internet, talk to human resources professionals to get solid data on what's current and what's emerging in pay and benefits packages for your area and line of work. You want to look progressive – but realistic.

Remember, getting the right deal *is* a process and it may take some time. Therefore, don't be willing to jump at the first thing that's thrown your way – even if you desperately need the job. Jumping at something often leads to unhappiness in the mid- to long-term. A key skill of a professional is to be able to think quickly and to identify the pros and cons, short- and long-term, of an offer. If you've established your minimum and maximum wants and gives ahead of time, the negotiation process actually is much easier to successfully manage.

5. **Play Poker** – Compensation experts also suggest that you use your poker face during this process. Whatever nervous twitches or tendencies you have, be aware of them now so you don't default to them during the negotiation process. When you're nervous, do you raise your eyebrows or bite your lower lip? Do you bounce your knee or pick your fingernails? You want to convince those with whom you're negotiating, that this process isn't a nerve-wracking experience for you, but

rather a business deal to be approached logically. You will project a more professional image if you can negotiate your own compensation package from a non-emotional, professional perspective.

6. **Be Ready to Walk** - If you don't like what they're offering, be ready to walk – and do it professionally. If they don't meet your minimums, you'd better walk, or you won't be happy. If you believe you're getting backed into a corner and will have to start giving or caving in to hold onto your minimum (floor) deal, ask for something you know is a "giveaway" for them, (i.e., extra vacation, enhanced title, etc.) The objective here is to try to *force* them to give you something if you're going to have to *give* something yourself. This way, you win: you get your floor deal with something extra – and they win: they *got* you.

Leaders who succeed take control of their lives. They don't wait for others to hand them opportunities and they don't believe they're owed anything. Leaders figure out what kind of glasscutter, or skills, they need to cut through or around their current obstacles.

Tip # 10 - Get Over the Glass Ceiling Thing

Are you stuck below the glass ceiling and can't cut through? Have men and management been holding you back? Did your "ex" prevent you from pursuing your career dreams? Does being a mom hold you back from taking leadership positions?

Get over it. Stop the victim thing. Unless someone has held you hostage, threatened you or your family with bodily harm or with some other dubious act, the jobs you've had and the relationships you've been in have been choices you've made. You were the person who chose to stick with it. You were the one who chose *not* to leave.

I know glass ceilings exist in many organizations. But if you focus more on being female in a male-dominated organization – or for that matter – male in a female-dominated organization, that's all you'll see and you won't see the other opportunities open to you to advance your career.

Besides, the victimization attitude does not equate to leadership – unless you're the lead victim. If in fact you were sabotaged at work, that was a really sleazy obstacle you had to overcome. There are many people out there who would rather sabotage some-one else than focus their energies on doing good. Those "geniuses" who develop and disperse computer viruses are classic exam-ples.

However, if you have been sabotaged, deal with it. Then move on. If you keep won-dering why others held you back, if you keep licking your wounds, or if you keep plotting your revenge, you're focusing your energies and skills in a way that serves no good – for you or anyone else. Your ener-gies should be focused on addressing any loose ends, and then on moving forward. A leadership mindset is not stuck in the past or wound-licking. It is intent on moving for-ward. You can't lead when you're looking backward.

> *...the jobs you've had and the relationships you've been in have been choices you've made. You were the person who chose to stick with it. You were the one who chose not to leave.*

No One Owes You

Men and other women aren't holding you back. You're choosing not to move on. If you have the skills and abilities to do the job, there's very little to hold you back. Yeah, I know that currently only a few women are CEOs in Fortune 500 companies. But there are growing numbers of women holding board positions in Fortune 500 firms, as well as others who are starting their own businesses. These women business-owners realized they were not going to achieve their goals with their previous employers, and took a huge leap of faith – a leap of faith in themselves. They started their own companies to provide themselves, and others, with an alternative opportunity and an alternative organization within which to achieve their leadership success.

In the Town Hall Forum conducted at the May 2002 National Association for Female Executives (NAFE) Annual Conference, 48% of the 400 participants indicated that "risk-taking and thinking out of the box had been the most important factor for the growth of their careers."

These women didn't wait for someone else to hand them an opportunity. They were willing to take risks and to take control of their own lives. They didn't all start their own companies, but they *did* take control of their own careers.

I shared this story in my **Manager's Corner** column a few years ago:

While working with a client recently, the conversation turned to the business partner who was absent. That partner had recently been described by one of the employees as "an unhappy person." The partner I was meeting with asked, "What can I do to make him happy? I've tried altering his responsibilities these past few years, and nothing appeals to him." My response was "You can't make him happy. He has to do that for himself."

In my first job out of college, I learned from my boss that I was the person who was responsible for determining my personal and professional happiness. I had been angry with my boss because he hadn't been helping me identify my next career move. He had simply looked at me and basically said, "Liz, no one else is responsible for making you happy. Don't look to someone else to find you a better job, or find you one that pays more or has better benefits. Most importantly, no one else but you can define what type of work will make you happy." It was one of those life-changing moments. From that moment on, I stopped looking to others to open doors for me. I'd look for the keys and open them myself.

If you view the job you have or the one you anticipate accepting as nothing more than a paycheck, how long will you be happy working there? If you're not happy with the type of work you do, why not expand into something you truly enjoy? Your happiness, as well as your productivity, will increase.

To help with this, review your working years. Identify all of those jobs or tasks you had that you enjoyed. What was the common thread among them? Identify the common thread and look for it in your current or next job. That thread can be the key to your personal and professional happiness. As an example, the jobs I enjoyed were: teaching aerobics in college, training other aerobics instructors, and teaching college. Now, I enjoy corporate training, consulting, and keynoting. Can you see the pattern? I thrive on training, teaching, being in control,

and being in front of people. I can't help it.
It's who I am, so I've made it what I do.

What is the common theme to your most
enjoyable jobs? You owe it to yourself to
identify what will make you happy.

> *No one else is responsible for making
> you happy. Don't look to someone else
> to find you a better job, or find you one
> that pays more or has better benefits.
> Most importantly, no one else but you
> can define what type of work will
> make you happy.*

Stop Whining

No one likes whiners. I've yet to hear anyone tell me after a training session or speech
that they like working with whiners. No one
likes listening to them or being around
them. Most people ignore them, walk away
from them, and lose respect for them.
Whining only serves as a way for a whiner
to drone on about her victimization.

How often have you ignored, walked away from, or lost respect for someone who took responsibility for a tough situation – whether it was hers to handle or not? I thought so. Me too. It sounds harsh, I know, but not many people really care how hard your life is or how hard you work. We all have challenges and we all believe we work hard. So drop it.

Also, no one, least of all the guys, wants to hear how cold you think the air conditioning is or how sore your feet are. Dress appropriately. Drink some hot tea if you're cold, but quit whining. Do your job. Control your life. Make things happen for yourself. It's no one else's responsibility.

Abide by the House Rules

The mindset that others are holding you back or are somehow denying something that's owed to you is a mindset I see in many women *and* men. It's a victim's mindset. A victim's mindset is a passive mindset. Victims in this sense believe they have no control over their own lives and are at the mercy of others. They passively participate in life and in their careers – waiting for others to offer them opportunities.

Because this mindset is present in many of my client organizations, I discuss the importance of an organizational Values Statement with just about every client or group I meet. Here's why: When a Values Statement is written well, it becomes a key guiding force in behavior and thinking for an organization. I call it the organization's "House Rules." Basically, the Values Statement defines how the organization, and everyone who works for it, will behave while conducting business. A Values Statement serves the same purpose for an organization as the "House Rules" when you visit someone's home. Certain behaviors are acceptable while you're there and others are not. A Values Statement outlines what behaviors and qualities the organization will expect from its employees and what it will exhibit as an organization (i.e., exceptional product and service quality, total customer satisfaction, employee and co-worker respect, continuous learning and improvement, fair pricing, fair profits, etc.). So if you don't like the way the organization "behaves" or what it expects of you – leave. No one is forcing you to stay.

I recently discussed this issue with a roomful of government employees with an average time on the job of over 20 years. They were moaning and groaning about management (By the way, many of their gripes had merit). However, I told them, "If you cashed your last paycheck, that was your default signal, you agree to continue to abide by the House Rules. If the House Rules say, 'Present positive, helpful attitudes,' that's a required behavior you must exhibit while you're working here. If you don't want to behave in this way any longer – fine. Then all you need to do is leave and work for an organization with a Values Statement that's more comfortable for you. I don't care if you only have three more years until retirement and you'll lose a good bit of your pension if you leave now. Your job, as long as you keep cashing those paychecks, is to abide by the House Rules and support this organization and its customers to the best of your abilities. If you can't do that, it's time for you to leave."

Move Up, Over, Out, Up, and Back In

At this same presentation, I also told the participants that if they're facing a tough hierarchy, they should take a lateral move, then move up in the new department or organization, and then lateral back into their former organization. A woman in the audience became angry when I gave that advice. She stated that if no one stayed to "fight the fight," women would never be able to break through the glass ceiling. She was right. But how long are you willing to beat your head against the ceiling from below and hope you can push your way up – against the system in place?

I realized she had missed my point, so I clarified it a bit. Because of the laws of physics, it's easier to break through a barrier from the top because the force of gravity will help. This same theory applies in the professional world. It's easier to break the glass ceiling barriers from the top than to push through from the bottom. Once you're above the barrier, you have much more influence and ability to change the barrier "laws." You also have a great deal more leverage to pull others up to where you are. Pulling someone up is much easier than pushing from below.

After clarifying this point, I asked the audience to individually decide: *Do you want to spend your time sitting in your current position pushing on the glass ceiling from be-*

low? Or, do you want to continue to gain skills, experience, pay increases, and promotions in different departments or even outside your current organization?

If you choose the latter, you're better positioned to move back into your starting organization at a level above the glass ceiling. Then you can really make a difference. However, you can only do this if you're willing to take a risk. You may need to change positions and to change organizations to gain the experience and skills that will allow you to move back in at a level above the glass ceiling. When you're above the ceiling, you can more easily change the rules.

What's Your Priority?

A former senior partner in the firm told me years ago, "You don't have challenges, you have priorities. Choose your priority and stick by your choice."

Margaret Duncan,
Financial Analyst

If you believe you're stuck and can't move up any further, it may be time to leave and to find a position that better meets your personal and professional needs. *But what about the money? I can't make this kind of money elsewhere!*

What's your priority? If it's the money, then zip your lips and stay where you are. If it's working with an organization that provides greater professional challenges with less pay, then move there. But stop blaming others and claiming victimization because you're not happy with your current position.

Leaders aren't victims. They don't wait for others to hand them opportunities and they don't believe they're owed anything. Leaders figure out what kind of glasscutter, or skills, they need to cut through or around their current obstacles. They make themselves happy first, enjoy their professional challenges, enjoy what they're doing, and realize they have to make things happen for themselves. But first they figure out what they want.

What's your priority?

Impress me by challenging me! Tell me you aspire to something greater! I will challenge you back and look for your creativity, persistence, and tenacity in solving problems, and getting things done. Work to separate yourself from the crowd. But always remember, business is a risk...there are no guarantees. Most people want to be safe and not assume this risk. Most importantly...don't play the victim!
Dan Fisher, President & CEO –
D.L. Martin Company

*Be a professional equal because of your
brainpower, not your sex. You were
born a woman, be proud of it. You're
becoming the professional and the
leader you want to be by choice
and hard work.*

Tip # 11 - Be an Equal – Not a Belle – Blend "Woman-ness" with Business

Have you heard the saying:
> *Look like a woman;*
> *Act like a lady;*
> *Think like a prophet; and*
> *Work like a horse.*

I think many of us women were raised with this philosophy as a guiding principle. However, when taken to an extreme, the problem with acting like a lady when we're in professional situations is that we tend to:

- expect to be taken care of;
- mother others instead of develop them;
- defer to men;
- back away from confrontation and conflicts;
- let others speak over us or on our behalf; and,
- act as if we're better seen and not heard.

Let's embellish this a bit to be clear, because so often, this is the part of my talks and training programs that audience members seem to appreciate the most – *The Basic How-To's*.

Your Presence Is the Key

Powerful people take up physical space.
Deb Sofield,
Professional Speech Coach

Control Your Space - Whether it's your personal space or your physical space, you need to control it. Take it so someone else doesn't take it from you. It's a control thing; it's a power thing.

Deb Sofield, a professional speaking coach from Greenville, South Carolina says, *"Powerful people stand up straight and look you in the eye. Powerful people take up physical space."*

Men have a tendency to spread out – both physically and with their "space." Physically, men will spread their legs, whether standing or sitting, and take up space. When they sit, they often cross their legs and angle their top leg out and take up space. We women cross our legs and even cross our ankles to be modest and take up less space. Men sit back and spread their arms out across the backs of chairs – again claiming space. Women will "scootch" over and give up space to others. Now don't spread your legs and start to sprawl all over the place in an attempt to "claim space." Just don't be the first one to give up space each and every time.

If you have to make space for another person, as you start to move over, look at the person next to you and ask him to move over a bit as you move over a bit. If he does move, wonderful. If he doesn't move, stop, look him in the eyes, and ask him again as you start to lean to move again. If he still doesn't move, scootch into his space and take some of it. Then, just act as if you belong there. Don't apologize for squishing him. He had the chance to move and didn't. Be polite but be firm.

The physical space you occupy also needs to project "professionalism" and "leadership" ability. Therefore, as mentioned before, control your office space. Your office shouldn't be the place for those trinkets and knick-knacks you couldn't find a place for in your house. Of course you can personalize your space with family pictures, but keep the "girly" decorations under control, and keep your makeup, extra shoes, other pieces of clothing and personal hygiene items in drawers or cabinets.

Men also take up space with their offices and work areas, yet they typically only furnish their offices minimally. They usually only use a desk, a few chairs, and bookshelves – powerful-looking furniture. Men typically don't keep filing cabinets in their offices, because stereotypically men don't file; the administrative staff – i.e., women – does. Women, on the other hand, usually keep filing cabinets close at hand to minimize the time needed to get to them.

If you keep filing cabinets in your office or work area, keep only a few. Don't line entire walls in your office with them or your space will start looking like the filing room. Don't top them with a menagerie of plants and knick-knacks. Do use them as added powerful pieces of furniture by placing framed awards or certificates of recognition on top of them.

Finally, your vehicle is also "your space." Clients may walk by your car in parking lots or they may ride with you to lunch. Do you have makeup in the cup holders for those on-the-way-to-work applications or is your car relatively neat and clean? Keep it clean – or at least trash-free.

Be aware. Be professional. Control your space.

Make an Entrance – If there is one thing I've learned since I started training, consulting and speaking, it's that: *You're always "ON."* Whether you're in front of the audience, waiting to "go on," in the back of the room drinking coffee, or parking your car in the parking lot, you have to always be "a professional." If not, some who see you will remember that just 15 minutes before you acted like a jerk towards them in the parking lot. Now, here you are claiming to be a professional. It won't work. Their first impression of you will carry over.

Because you're always "on," make an entrance that is confident. Hold your head up. Scan the room and make eye contact. Approach, greet, and shake hands with those you haven't seen in awhile. Don't keep your head ducked and scurry to the first open chair. Look confident and ready; not frightened and hurried.

There's a rule of thumb that says, "We make our first impression on people within the first 90 seconds. People will then spend the next two to three minutes affirming or disaffirming that initial impression." Therefore make your first impression a good one.

Make Eye Contact – When you look down, your head tends to tilt down. As your head tilts down, your shoulders will often slump forward slightly. This is what I call *The Young Princess Di* look. Remember when we were first introduced to Princess Diana? The Royal Family was announcing Diana and Prince Charles's engagement. In most of the photographs and taped footage of that event, Diana's head was tilted down. She raised only her eyes and peered at the reporters through her bangs. I remember thinking, "Oh that poor girl." I think anyone who saw her at that time just wanted to comfort her.

However, after she had faced considerable marital struggles and had gained self-confidence, her head was up, she made strong eye contact with her fans, and she appeared more self-assured.

Often, like her, many of us will keep our heads tilted down, and only raise our eyes to make intermittent eye contact with others. When I ask client groups what this type of body language conveys, I'm consistently told that particular physical carriage screams, "Insecurity; lack of confidence." I'm not an expert on body language nor are any of my client groups, yet to all of us, that head posture sends the same "insecurity and non-leadership material" message.

When you make eye contact, hold the contact for about three to five seconds before looking away. Eye contact shorter than that and you will look shifty; any longer, and you will appear a bit too intense.

Have a Leadership Posture – Growing up, my mom made my sisters and me (I'm the tallest at 5'11") stand against a wall to feel how a truly straight posture felt. She instilled in us at an early age that there's nothing sillier than a tall woman stooping over in an attempt to look shorter. *Hello, you're almost six foot tall!* Stooping is *not* going to make you look shorter. It just makes you look like a tall person with poor posture. Besides, a strong posture enhances your leadership and confidence image.

Don't Pick Your Fingernails – If you tend to pick at your fingernails, it's not only rude to do basic grooming in front of others, it forces you to keep your head down and it limits your ability to make or maintain eye contact. Besides, you look insecure and more interested in your poor manicure than the real issue at hand. Be aware of your picking habits.

Stand Up When Introduced or When Someone Enters the Room – I often see women remain seated as a prospective male client walks into a room or a new male colleague enters the room. Men stand up; you should too. If you stay seated, it's just another subtle way you're indicating to others in the room that you're "different"; you're a girl. Participate in professional protocol. It's polite. It's professional. It's "The Rule."

When I mentioned this idea in a presentation I gave recently to a predominantly male audience, several male audience members stood up and applauded. After my presentation, they told me this behavior, by some of their female colleagues, is one of their pet peeves. Their female colleagues remain seated in meetings or at professional functions and expect to be treated differently for that one instance, but demand equality in all others. Be consistent. Be a professional.

Limit the luggage – Pack for the event, not the entire journey. Be aware of the "luggage" that is hanging off the back of your chair, that is under your chair, or that is entwined around your ankles. It could inhibit your ability to easily stand and move to greet someone.

If possible, don't carry a big purse *and* a briefcase. Men don't carry purses *and* briefcases. They carry one briefcase which makes it easy for them to move around. When you start lugging around too much baggage, you look like a bag lady and become down right dangerous as your luggage bangs into people as you rush in and out of meetings.

If you sling your purse or briefcase over your shoulder (as I do), be very careful and control its "swing" potential. At a conference recently, I sat in the last row in the end seat. A woman walked passed me and "beaned" me on the head with the purse slung over her shoulder. She didn't even realize what she'd done and just continued on her way. Believe me, I wasn't too pleased, as her purse had some weight to it and carried quite a punch!

There are great combination purse/briefcase pieces available that can carry all of the essentials necessary in a purse, as well as your files, laptop, PDA, cell phone, etc. Carry one bag if possible. This lets you deal with less "stuff" and gives you more time to focus on getting the job done.

Finally, in crowded areas, carry your purse/briefcase in your left hand at thigh level. They're much less dangerous there, and you'll always be ready to shake hands without the awkward pause while you shift bags to free up your right hand.

Don't Wait to Be Introduced - Take the initiative to introduce yourself. Ask others for their names. If they don't state them immediately, look them in the eyes as you ask them their names. This shows assertiveness, energy, and interest. If you wait to be introduced, you are waiting for chivalry to take hold and that's not what's important now. If your hosts fail to introduce you, do it yourself. If they do take the initiative, great! That shows courtesy and professionalism on their part.

Take the initiative to introduce yourself as a professional.

Initiate Handshakes - Initiate handshakes, and I mean real, full-hand, firm, professional handshakes. Not the southern belle, fingertip, limp-wristed kind. Not the dead fish, low energy, no squeeze, touch-of-the-hand kind. Not the two-handed hold. And not a knuckle-buster.

Just grasp the person's hand firmly and give a slight squeeze as you exchange introductions. There's no need to pump your joined hands up and down repeatedly as you talk; you're not pumping a well.

A handshake is one of the ways you have to make a solid first impression as a confident professional. You won't get comfortable with shaking hands until you start doing it regularly. Besides, while shaking hands, you've just "bought" a bit of time to look at the other person.

Make solid eye contact. Then listen to hear her name. Say her name as you greet her, "It's nice to meet you Ms. McHenry." Shake hands. Then, start a conversation. Without the few added seconds required to complete a professional handshake, we often will not take the time to listen to a person's name and repeat it to lock it into our memories. Instead we just jump into a conversation, and then walk away not remembering who we just met.

Initiate handshakes with men and other women. Typically we wait for men or other women to reach for our hand. If they don't, we women often skip the handshake altogether. When I included this comment in a speech to a group of Woman Insurance Underwriters, one of the attendees said, "But I feel uncomfortable initiating handshakes with men. I think it's their responsibility to initiate it." Bingo! You're expecting them to be chivalrous, yet you don't want to be viewed as a woman, but as one of their peers. You're playing both sides of the fence again and that's not fair. You get what you deserve. Do you want to be treated differently or as a professional equal?

Business Cards – Have you ever watched a woman dig into her purse and then into her wallet or her business card holder just to find a card to pass to someone? She looked rather disorganized, didn't she? If just handing out a business card is such a hassle, what will she do with a large, confusing client account?

Have your business cards easily available. Have some on your desk; tuck some into your suit coat pocket, slacks pocket, or in an easy-to-access, outside pocket of your purse or briefcase. Wherever you carry them, have the cards positioned with the writing facing the inside of your pocket or purse. This will allow you to put your hand in, draw out a card, and present it with the front facing the recipient. You won't have to flip it around. However, make sure you have a separate location to keep any cards you receive from others so you don't mix them in with yours and present someone else's card by mistake.

Use them as an introductory tool. When calling on a prospective client, as you tell the office receptionist the person you're coming to see, hand the receptionist one of your cards. This will enable the receptionist to see and hear your name immediately. The receptionist can then take your card and give it to the person you're to meet to alert her that you're waiting.

Remember to carry more cards than you think you'll need. You don't want to run out. Finally, check the cards regularly to ensure you toss out any that are dog-eared or dirty.

Open Doors for Others – If you get to a door first and you're with a male colleague, don't revert to being a southern belle and wait for him to open the door for you. You open it. Then gesture to him to step up in front of you. Many men won't or will appear uncomfortable, but you're maintaining your equal position. If he does appear uncomfortable, simply step through the door yourself and hold it open until he grabs it. However, if a man does open the door for you, simply say, "Thank you" and walk through. That was kind of him. Acknowledge it and move through. Don't be insulted by his perceived chivalry. He was being kind.

The point is: It's simply polite to open doors for others – women or men. It's also polite if someone opens a door for you. But don't wait for it, don't expect it, or heaven forbid, don't be offended by it.

Control Your Head – This was another, "Oh-my-gosh" insight for me. Deb Sofield also advises her female clients to be aware of their head tilts and nodding. According to Deb, women nod their heads to indicate to the speaker that they're listening or that they understand what is being said. Men don't nod unless they agree. Therefore, men believe we women are agreeing with them, when we're only trying to indicate, *"We hear you."* Also, women tend to tilt their heads as they listen to others. Men don't.

Hold your head up straight. It's more powerful and sends a message that you're in control and that you're listening.

Control Your Smiles – Women also tend to smile more than men, particularly when they're trying to appease or to keep others calm. Men don't. When a woman wants to impress someone or appear "approachable" she smiles. To many, this appears weak or a sign of submission. People who are confident smile when appropriate.

Control Your Voice – Pay attention to good female television show hosts or news reporters. Their voices aren't typically high and "girly;" they're a bit lower. They sound professional and confident.

If your voice is weak or high-pitched, project your voice from the center of your mouth. This will help drop the pitch just slightly. Don't speak from the back of your throat or you'll sound gravelly and fake. Project from the center of your mouth – right from the highest part of your mouth

cavity. If you do, this subtle change in pro-
jection will drop your vocal tone slightly.
You'll sound more confident and less
"girly."

Your Clothes Are Your Tools

Have you ever noticed in most classic mov-
ies, whenever the leading man and leading
lady have to run away to escape the villain,
the woman trips on her high heels, falls, and
twists an ankle? So the big strong man has
to stop, run back, pick her up, and carry her
to safety.

Ughh, I hate those scenes! What do you
think of a woman who doesn't know enough
to take off her spikes so she can run like
hell? I don't know about you, but if she
can't figure out that minor detail, she's not
leadership material in my book. Or, worse
yet, if she's more concerned with looking
good than getting the job done, she's really
not on my leadership radar screen.

If you want to look like a girl, just wear
spiked heels when you've got a lot of walking to do, when *you know* you're going to a
client site and will need to climb over

things, when you need to walk on a produc-tion floor, or get in and out of high–riding vehicles. Your shoes and your gait can serve as a neon sign that screams, "Woman in heels! Woman in heels!"

If others have to help you climb over stuff or get in and out of vehicles because of your shoes, you're reinforcing your "girly" image by your inability to keep up. Your team and clients have just stopped thinking of you as a leader and are now viewing you as a fe-male who needs help because you're a girl with "girly" clothes. You've just shifted roles. You're inconsistent. Wear the ap-propriate shoes and clothes for the job you need to do.

Also, dress appropriately for the culture. You can certainly add accessories with some flare to express yourself. But, choose clothes that compliment your body type without becoming the focus in and of them-selves. Your clothes should frame you nicely – like a picture frame. Your clothes are not *the* focus; they're background. You want people focused on *you* and what you have to say – not what you're wearing. Therefore, buy the classic styles that look professional, feminine, but not "frou-frouey." Besides, they won't go out of style as quickly. View them as an investment – a professional investment.

Finally, we've all heard that we should dress for the position and responsibilities we want. The reason for this is to make it easy for others to *see* us in the role we want. If we look the part, it can help others put us in that role. However, do this within reason. If dressing for the position you want causes you to dress in a manner that inhibits your ability to do the job you're currently required to fulfill, dress appropriately for the current job. Remember, you do have a job to do.

Control the distractions. If you want to be viewed as a leader, it helps to look like one. So long, heavy makeup; so long, overly flashy clothes; so long, cleavage. These comments may be too restricting, depending upon the organization you're leading, but for the vast majority of businesses and government agencies, when a woman has on heavy makeup, it doesn't take long to become obsessed with watching her to see when her eyelashes are going to get stuck together. When your focus is on a woman's makeup, her short skirt, or her cleavage, it's hard to concentrate on what she's actually saying. Her "girly" appearance has made it much harder for you to focus on her as a leader.

Similarly, control distracting jewelry, particularly if you have a tendency to twirl your rings and earrings or twist your necklaces around your fingers. When I was in my final semester of college, my Communications team and I had to give a presentation to our classmates that would be taped. Before we were able to watch ourselves on tape, our classmates had the opportunity to provide comments on the strength of our presentations. My team and I had prepared thoroughly and presented our material without a hitch, so when it came time for the class to critique my team, I was waiting for them to say, "Incredible!" or "Well researched." We received good comments, but several students also said, "Liz kept twirling the ring on her pinky finger and it drove us nuts!" I was floored! *How petty of them! Who cares about my ring? Didn't they pay attention to the presentation? Gosh, they were so immature!*

However, when we watched the tape, I started to shrink in my chair. I couldn't stop watching myself twirl my ring. I hadn't been aware of it while presenting. Yet, there I was, twirling and twirling away. Man, was it annoying! Then it finally dawned on me. I had created my own distraction. I had prevented the audience from getting the message. They weren't petty and they were not picking on me. They were cluing me in.

When you pick at your cuticles, twirl your jewelry, twist your hair – or for men – jiggle keys or coins in your pockets, you look nervous or anxious. It unsettles others. Just watch how others react as you sit and bounce your leg or pick your cuticles.

Be aware of your dangly jewelry and other detractors, because they'll be just that: detractors – self-generated detractors.

> *...when a woman has on heavy make-up, it doesn't take long to become obsessed with watching her to see when her eyelashes are going to get stuck together. When your focus is on a woman's makeup, her short skirt, or her cleavage, it's hard to concentrate on what she's actually saying.*

You Can't Be the Smelly One

When talking about this book with my brother, Bill, I mentioned I was going to include a section on being aware of how much perfume one wears. His comment was, *"It's not how much – NO perfume! If it's not the right scent, it's an irritant. We don't need to smell you."*

When he said that, it dawned on me that working with someone who wears a perfume I don't like is no different than working with someone with body odor or bad breath. If the smell – body odor, bad breath, or perfume – is offensive, it's offensive. It *is* an irritant and distracts from my ability to stay focused and productive. Therefore, it becomes a production issue.

In my 20 years of consulting and training, it's amazing how many times the issue of telling a co-worker he or she has body odor or bad breath has come up with client groups. It's a difficult issue to address with the "offender", but it needs to be addressed. Because, as I've noted above, if the odor is an irritant and distracts from your or your team's ability to get the job done, it's a production issue; therefore, it's an issue you need to address.

Also, there are numerous people who suffer with allergies and who are allergic to scents. If you wear a perfume that is causing your team members' eyes to water and their noses to run, you're really creating an obstacle for their performance, and that's simply not fair to them.

If you want to be a professional and a leader, don't create smelly obstacles for your colleagues to work around. A leader's responsibility is to minimize obstacles, not create them.

And PLEASE – Don't Resort to Your Womanly Wiles!

I didn't think I'd have to discuss the inappropriateness of flirting in the workplace, but it did come up in some of my survey responses as a definite "No-No," so I'll address it.

One of my contributors referred me to a book written recently that identified "Needed Skills" for women to succeed in the business world. The book suggested using your "womanly skills" to get ahead.

The experts in favor of this tactic believe that flirting is somehow "smart business," politically correct, and a means to build better business relationships between women and men in the workplace. I disagree – vehemently. Have you ever worked with a flirt – someone who uses her or his sexuality to get ahead? I have. I've seen it ruin office morale, teamwork, and careers. Neither the men nor women who subscribe to this practice earn respect from their peers, managers, clients, or colleagues. Your peers and managers are looking for integrity and brainpower, not notches on a bedpost.

I discussed this topic with several of my contributors. One of my male contributors is a good-looking man who has had female co-workers and employees comment on his looks. He shared his tactic for dealing with workplace flirts: *"I'm not going to go there. It's very easy to send out the signals that I'm not interested. If you don't emit, you don't get."*

Don't flirt. Don't demean yourself, your professionalism, and your hard work. Be a professional equal because of your brainpower, not your sex. You were born a woman, be proud of it. You're becoming the professional and the leader you want to be by choice and hard work.

Stand tall. Hold your head up. Know your stuff. Project your confidence and let others see you as the powerful person you are.

Be the professional you are. Be the leader you are. Be the success you are. Then you won't have to worry about being treated like a girl, because you won't let 'em!

Good luck and don't let 'em treat you like a girl.

What Do Women Really Want?

Young King Arthur was ambushed and imprisoned by the monarch of a neighboring kingdom. The monarch could have killed him, but was moved by Arthur's youth and ideals. So the monarch offered him freedom, as long as he could answer a question that had caused the monarch endless difficulties. Arthur would have a year to figure out the answer; if, after a year, he still had no answer, he would be put to death.

The question: *What do women really want?*

Such a question would perplex even the most knowledgeable man, and, to young Arthur, it seemed an impossible query. But, since it was better than death, he accepted the monarch's proposition to have an answer by year's end. He returned to his kingdom and began to poll everybody: the princess, the prostitutes, the priests, the wise men, the court jester. He spoke with everyone, but no one could give him a satisfactory answer. Many people advised him to consult the old witch; only she would know the answer. The price would be high. The witch was famous throughout the kingdom for the exorbitant fees she exacted.

The last day of the year arrived and Arthur had no alternative but to talk to the witch. She agreed to answer his question, but he'd have to accept her price first: The old witch wanted to marry Gawain, the most noble of the Knights of the Round Table and Arthur's closest friend! Young Arthur was horrified. She was hunchbacked and hideous, had only one tooth, smelled like sewage, and made obscene noises. He had never encountered such a repugnant creature. He refused to force his friend to marry her and have to endure such a burden.

Gawain, upon learning of the proposal, spoke with Arthur. He told him that nothing was too big a sacrifice compared to Arthur's life and the preservation of the Round Table. Hence, their wedding was proclaimed, and the witch answered Arthur's question thus: *What a woman really wants is to be in charge of her own life.*

Everyone instantly knew that the witch had uttered a great truth and that Arthur's life would be spared. And so it was. The neighboring monarch granted Arthur total freedom.

What a wedding Gawain and the witch had! Arthur was torn between relief and anguish. Gawain was proper as always, gentle and courteous. The old witch put her worst manners on display and generally made everyone very uncomfortable.

The honeymoon hour approached. Gawain, steeling himself for a horrific experience, entered the bedchamber. But what a sight awaited him! The most beautiful woman he'd ever seen stood before him! The astonished Gawain asked what had happened. The beauty replied that since he had been so kind to her when she'd appeared as a witch, she would henceforth be her horrible, deformed self half the time, and the other half, she would be her beautiful maiden self. Which would he want her to be during the day, and which during the night?

What a cruel question! Gawain pondered his predicament. During the day, a beautiful woman to show off to his friends, but at night, in the privacy of his home, an old witch? Or would he prefer having by day a hideous witch, but by night a beautiful woman with whom to enjoy his personal life?

What would you do? What Gawain chose follows below, but don't read it until you've made your own choice.

***

Noble Gawain replied that he would let her choose for herself. Upon hearing this, she announced that she would be beautiful all the time, because he had respected her enough to let her be in charge of her own life.

What is the moral of this story?

If a woman doesn't get her own way, things are going to get ugly!

The above is a modernized version of Geoffrey Chaucer's "The Wife of Bath's Tale" from the Canterbury Tales. *The author of this version is unknown.*

Conclusion

Control over our own lives is something we often hand over to others. This book's purpose is to help you become aware of some of the ways you might be doing just that. It's your life. Take control of it. Become the leader, become the professional, become the person you want to be.

By the way, if you know the woman in Albuquerque, please buy her a copy of this book and tell her "Thanks." She's helped me clue in other women (and men) on what we need to do to attain our leadership success.

Please feel free to contact me at:
info@liz-weber.com or 41 South Antrim Way, Greencastle, PA 17225-1519, to comment on how this book could be improved. Also, I'd like to hear your thoughts and stories of leadership success and how you've learned how to not let 'em treat you like a girl!

Best of Luck - Liz

About the Author

Growing up the youngest of thirteen children (seven brothers and five sisters) of entrepreneurial parents, Liz learned early that in order to be included and to be treated as an equal, she had to pitch in and help get things done. Throughout her professional career, Liz has held positions heavily populated by men and has worked with a clientele (i.e., business owners, manufacturers, military personnel, senior foreign service officers) that has been dominated by men. In order to fit in and succeed, she needed to be viewed as an equal – and not as a girl. That meant she had to act as an equal, pitch in, and help get things done.

Liz Weber is the President of Weber Business Services, LLC (WBS), a management consulting and training firm, as well as the president of a commercial real estate development firm. Liz holds degrees in International Business (The George Washington University – M.B.A.; University of Wisconsin – B.B.A). She has traveled and worked in over 20 countries with small, medium, and large organizations. With 20 years' experience, Liz works with clients to develop growth strategies that are cohesive, complementary, and clearly aligned with the organization's long-term goals.

Her company's strategic planning and leadership development programs help everyone in an organization identify how he or she fits into and affects the organization's success. By teaching the clients' employees "The Business" and clearly developing and communicating "The Plan," Liz and her team are able to more quickly help clients achieve measurable improvements and establish employee commitment to organizational strategies and initiatives.

Liz has personally aided many clients in developing strategic plans; writing business and marketing plans; developing policy and procedures manuals; and designing and presenting numerous employee and leadership development training programs. One client has stated: "Liz's business experience and depth of knowledge are apparent. She has an exceptional instructional and consultation style."

With a professional background that includes extensive exposure to the international business and governmental arenas, Liz served as a contractor to the U.S. Department of State. She had management oversight responsibilities for activities in 139 countries. Liz has also served as a Faculty Associate with the Johns Hopkins University, The George Washington University, Penn State, and Wilson College.

In addition to her management and training consulting practice, Liz is also a professional speaker, author, and columnist. Her **Manager's Corner** column appears regularly in several publications. She is a member of the National Speakers Association, as well as the International Federation of Professional Speakers.

For more information, contact Weber Business Services, LLC, at *info@wbsllc.com* - *www.wbsllc.com* or call 717-597-8890.

Success Tools Available from the Author

MANAGER'S CORNER E-ZINE – FREE!

With this FREE monthly e-zine, you'll receive a copy of Liz's management article written for her *Manager's Corner* column. You're welcome to read the article, then include it in your organization's newsletters or publications. Please include the full attribution and send an e-mail to: *info@liz-weber.com* to let us know where you'll be reprinting the article. To subscribe, go to: *http://www.liz-weber.com/ezinearticle.htm*

ARE YOU LEADING? E-ZINE – $29.95

This e-zine is issued twice each month and is targeted to those in senior management (or those with senior management potential) who are seeking focused, concise ideas on how to develop their employees, develop their organizations, and develop themselves into the leaders of the future.

LEADING FROM THE MANAGER'S CORNER - ~~*$29.95*~~
 SPECIAL - $19.95
 (E-BOOK VERSION –
 ONLY $9.95)

You're leading, but they're not following. But how and where are you leading them? With ***Leading from the Manager's Corner,*** you can ensure you're leading everyone in the right direction. A collection of Liz's best articles from her ***Manager's Corner*** column, this book is for those who want to improve themselves and their leadership skills.

Product Order Form

Group pricing is available –
call 717-597-8890 for details.

Products	Qty	Price
MANAGER'S CORNER E-ZINE**	Free	Free
ARE YOU LEADING? E-ZINE ** - *$29.95 (24 issues)*		
LEADING FROM THE MANAGER'S CORNER - *Book - $19.95 each* - *E-Book - $9.95 each***		

Subtotal	$ _____
PA Residents add 6% Sales Tax	$ _____
Add Shipping & Handling - $3.50 - 1st item + $1.50 for each additional item	$ _____
Total:	$ _____

To Order Any of Liz's Products

*Order on-line at
www.liz-weber.com/products.htm
or
fax this form to 717-597-0535*

Name: _____

Phone: _____

Organization: _____

Address: _____

City/State/Zip: _____

E-Mail** (Required for e-zines and e-book):
_____

PAYMENT

☐ Check

Charge my account:
    ☐ Visa   ☐ MasterCard

Account #:_____

Exp. Date: _____

Signature: _____